ADVANCES IN FOREIGN POLICY ANALYSIS

Series Editor: Alex Mintz

Foreign policy analysis offers rich theoretical perspectives and diverse methodological approaches. Scholars specializing in foreign policy analysis produce a vast output of research. Yet, there were only very few specialized outlets for publishing work in the field. Addressing this need is the purpose of **Advances in Foreign Policy Analysis**. The series bridges the gap between academic and policy approaches to foreign policy analysis, integrates across levels of analysis, spans theoretical approaches to the field, and advances research utilizing decision theory, utility theory, and game theory.

Members of the Board of Advisors:

Published by Palgrave Macmillan:

Integrating Cognitive and Rational Theories of Foreign Policy Decision Making
Edited by Alex Mintz
Studies in International Mediation
Edited by Jacob Bercovitch
Media, Bureaucracies, and Foreign Aid: A Comparative Analysis of United States, the United Kingdom, Canada, France, and Japan
By Douglas A. Van Belle, Jean-Sébastien Rioux, and David M. Potter
Civil-Military Dynamics, Democracy, and International Conflict: A new Quest for International Peace
By Seung-Whan Choi and Patrick James

The Bush Administrations and Saddam Hussein

Deciding on Conflict

Alex Roberto Hybel
and
Justin Matthew Kaufman

THE BUSH ADMINISTRATIONS AND SADDAM HUSSEIN
© Alex Roberto Hybel, 2006.

First published in 2006 by
PALGRAVE MACMILLAN™
175 Fifth Avenue, New York, N.Y. 10010 and
Houndmills, Basingstoke, Hampshire, England RG21 6XS
Companies and representatives throughout the world.

PALGRAVE MACMILLAN is the global academic imprint of the Palgrave Macmillan division of St. Martin's Press, LLC and of Palgrave Macmillan Ltd. Macmillan® is a registered trademark in the United States, United Kingdom and other countries. Palgrave is a registered trademark in the European Union and other countries.

ISBN-13: 978–1–4039–7578–2
ISBN-10: 1–4039–7578–7

Library of Congress Cataloging-in-Publication Data

Hybel, Alex Roberto
    The Bush administrations and Saddam Hussein : deciding on conflict / by Alex Roberto Hybel and Matthew.
        p. cm.
    Includes bibliographical references and index.
    ISBN 1–4039–7578–7
        1. United States—Foreign relations—Iraq. 2. Iraq—Foreign relations—United States. 3. United States—Foreign relations—1989–
4. United States—Military policy. 5. Bush, George, 1924–
6. Bush, George W. (George Walker), 1946– 7. Hussein, Saddam, 1937– 8. Persian Gulf War, 1991. 9. Iraq War, 2003– I. Title.

E183.8.I57H93 2006
956.7044'32—dc22   2006046013

A catalogue record for this book is available from the British Library.

Design by Newgen Imaging Systems (P) Ltd., Chennai, India.

First edition: October 2006
10 9 8 7 6 5 4 3 2 1

Printed in the United States of America.

To
Barbara Peurifoy,
David, Karen, and Hanna Kaufman,
and Jeremy Whyman

CONTENTS

ACKNOWLEDGMENTS

Some scholars view teaching as the price they have to pay to do that which they really love: research. I am not one of them. My research informs my teaching, but it is through teaching that I often discern what I do not know. As a result, teaching has on more than one occasion dictated my research agenda. It is in the classroom, moreover, that I am repeatedly rewarded by the discovery of students with tremendous intellectual capacity and energy, waiting to encounter someone who will take them seriously and provide them with the opportunity to excel. It was after being exposed to Justin Matthew Kaufman's work in one of my seminars that I realized he was such a student. And that is how our research partnership started. Throughout the production of this book, Justin was the novice; his input, however, was so valuable that he merited full coauthorship.

Our work benefited from the research work and comments by a number of people. A few of them deserve special mention. Cassandra Lynn Waters, a Connecticut College alum now working in El Salvador, spent an entire semester looking into the foreign policy-making literature and summarizing some of the relevant findings. Stuart Vyse, William Rose, and the anonymous reviewers provided helpful suggestions. Students in my U.S. foreign policy classes identified data we had overlooked and alerted me to a number of mistakes and inconsistencies in earlier drafts. No one, however, contributed as extensively as Matthew Engel. Of no lesser value is Alexander L. George's contribution. Alex never read the manuscript, nor did he know that Justin and I were working on it; still, though some

23 years have gone by since he served as the director of my dissertation, his approach to the analyses of foreign policy-making remains deeply embedded in my mind. To all of them, many thanks.

Many others deserve my gratitude for a number of reasons. The wisdom, affection, and kindness of my wife Jan; the joyfulness of our two incredible daughters, Sabrina and Gabriela; the indulgent support of my in-laws, Barbara and Bob Peurifoy; and the unremitting love of my mother, Margarita, and her husband, Raymond Lonsbury, helped nurture my work.

As someone who for most of his early life did not develop deep roots in any one place, I tended to view comradeship as a temporary entitlement. This attitude began to change in Los Angeles, under John Odell and Margaret Gonder's caring guidance. It experienced its most consequential conversion during my years at Connecticut College, in the company of Robert Gay, Alexis Dudden, Fred Paxton, Sylvia Malizia, Lee Hisle, Julie Worthen, Maria Cruz Saco, Mary Devins, Susan and Jan Lindberg, Candace Howes, Stuart Vyse, Frank Graziano, Ybing Huang, Lan-Lan Wang, Tristan Borer, and John Nugent. For their friendship and the touch of levity they often add to my life, I am thankful.

One person deserves additional words of appreciation. More than two decades ago, while I was trying to complete my dissertation, my mother-in-law, Barbara Peurifoy, kindly volunteered to type and edit it. Since then, no one has helped me more, or could have been more patient in my writing endeavor, than Barbara. One particular instance is worth mentioning. After reading a passage that she found incomprehensible, she called and asked me to clarify it. For reasons unbeknownst to me (cockiness maybe), I said: "It is a complicated argument; people in my field will understand it." Calmly, she responded: "Alex, obviously I don't know the subject as well as you do, but I am an intelligent person. If I don't understand it, it means it is not written well." She was right. Since then, every time I write something of some significance, I ask myself: "Will it measure up to

Barbara's standards?" Despite her tenacity, I continue to make mistakes, but I am their sole owner. I dedicate this book to her.

Alex Roberto Hybel
Stonington, CT

One of my favorite songwriters once wrote of his success: "I find it hard to explain how I got here . . ." Having my name attached to this book gives me a new appreciation of the utter humility that a man must feel when he sings that line in front of sold-out arenas and stadiums.

For as long as I can remember, I have been something of a dreamer. In school my teachers reported on this behavior to my parents with phrases like "he has so much potential," or "he clearly has good ideas"; phrases that were inevitably followed by the less-than-flattering "but his head always seems to be elsewhere." Of course my head was always elsewhere; it was drawing blueprints for my next big idea. I have always believed the greatest achievements or ideas are those that are original, unique, and progressive in content. By now I have realized that the process of arriving at such thoughts is often, at best, unavailing.

Nonetheless, in the course of my pursuits, three people have seen my lofty goals and ideas as more than just extravagant dreams. In this forum I would like to simply recognize two of them by name— Noah Siegel and Alex Sandman. Your faith in me is my fuel for every day.

The third person is Alex Roberto Hybel. There are several good films that document the relationship between a student and a professor, that is, *Good Will Hunting, The Emperor's Club,* and *Dead Poets' Society.* Working with Alex while at Connecticut College and during the 18 months following my graduation felt nothing short of movie-like. Alex has been inspiring to me in the same way that the Robin Williams' character (John Keating) was inspiring to his students in *Dead Poets, Society.* In our regular meetings to discuss our respective responsibilities and the direction of this book, I had the rare opportunity to discuss any and every idea born in my mind with him, and have the ideas listened to and scrutinized. In my academic experience, a relationship of this nature between a student and a professor is rare, and I am grateful to have been lucky enough to cross paths with Alex. Thus, as per my acknowledgment, I thank the most inspirational professor of my academic life, Alex Roberto Hybel, for giving me the tools to think critically about the world of politics and foreign policy-making, and the confidence to voice those thoughts. I hope our paths cross many times in the future.

Justin Matthew Kaufman
New York, NY

FOREWORD
Ronald Steel

Should we expect the decision to go to war to be rational when so much else about human life is not? Of course we do expect this, and we are often disillusioned. This illuminating study of the two recent American wars in Iraq is a case in point. It asks why, and then demonstrates how; emotion rather than reason guided the decisions to go to war. In doing so it reminds us once again that even in the affairs of state, the heart has its reasons that reason does not know.

No activity of a state demands more of its citizens or evokes more fervent emotions than does war. Yet few are subject to less hard analysis by those who make the critical decisions. This distressing axiom is splendidly illustrated by Alex Hybel and Justin Kaufman. With precision and intellectual objectivity they demonstrate, on both a theoretical and a practical level, how emotion and wishful thinking supplanted rationality in the two Iraq wars.

War is, of course, always unpredictable, both in its course and in its consequences. For this reason those who embark upon it tread upon uncertain ground. They should be wary, but almost without exception the instigators of war are dramatically bold. They believe that they can control the consequences of their actions.

In defense of their bold actions they sometimes cite Clausewitz, who famously argued that war is the pursuit of politics by other means. But they do not take to heart the warning inherent in his famous dictum. If war is indeed the pursuit of politics, then it is obviously subject to all the irrationality, hyperbole, and dishonesty of the political arena. War is just as haphazard, unpredictable, and irrational as any other form of human behavior. History and literature are replete with examples.

Indeed it would be heroically difficult to prove the contrary. Yet such is our human proclivity to war—indeed our attraction to it—that we want to believe war occurs because the reasons for it are overwhelming and ineluctable—and even more, that the ultimate consequences can be known and controlled. If we did not naively believe this we might be less inclined to pursue it.

War is a staple of human behavior. It is doubtful that there has ever been a moment when it was not taking place somewhere or other on our planet. The scale varies according to the capacity of the participants. And the rationale depends on the usual factors of fear, greed, ambition, hate, opportunity, ignorance, and delusion, to name the most obvious.

In some cases wars seem to break out with stunning spontaneity, like powder kegs that apparently ignite on their own. But on closer inspection one notes that someone filled the powder kegs, or put them in a hazardous place, or inflated their importance. Powder kegs are often the pretext rather than the primary cause for war. Their significance usually lies not in the event itself, but rather in the reaction to it.

War is, by its very nature, never a one-sided affair. One side may initiate and the other side respond, but that is only the narrative part of the story. The more important question lies in why nations deliberately choose war and believe it will necessarily advance what they perceive to be their interests.

Some states are simply aggressive and seek continental or even global domination. This is an ambition that they usually describe in idealistic terms, such as "advancing civilization," "world order," and the like. More commonly, a state may launch a war for what its leaders assert to be "defensive" reasons.

Among these is the perceived need to attack before being attacked. While this is essentially an aggressive act, it is often justified by those who commit it as "preemption," or more vaguely as "preventive war." A particularly egregious example of this would be Nazi Germany's invasion of Poland and later of the Soviet Union.

The attacked nation may, indeed usually does, choose to respond in kind, and in this case a full-fledged war takes place. We then say that the nation being attacked is forced into fighting a defensive war. But of course not all nations respond to aggression by resisting their attacker. Some simply surrender.

That may be viewed as a cowardly reaction. It certainly is not considered to be heroic. But in some cases, of which history furnishes myriad examples, it may be deemed a practical way of dealing with overwhelming odds and making the best of a hopeless situation.

One variant for a weak state in the path of a powerful aggressor is to proclaim its neutrality and to be as unobtrusive and cooperative as possible. Such states in certain cases can be more useful to the aggressor as formal "neutrals" than as occupied territories. This was the path chosen by Sweden and Switzerland in World War II.

There is no all-purpose formula for explaining why nations launch aggressive wars or why they respond as they do to the threat (real, perceived, imagined, or manipulated) of aggression (actual, potential, or contrived) against them. This depends on the nature of the state, the psychology and ambitions of its leaders, and an assessment of the costs and benefits of going to war.

The human factor is clearly critical. Those in control of a state—whether elected, crowned, or self-appointed—make the decision between war and peace. The general assumption is they do so for reasons that appear to be rational to them, at least at the time. For its part the public, which in a democracy must theoretically approve the decision to go to war, has to be persuaded that its leaders are reacting rationally and in the public's general interest.

This is how it is supposed to work. But the burden of proof is greater on the elected leaders when the war is aggressive rather than defensive—that is to say, if it is a war of choice rather than a war of necessity, a war the nation launches rather than one it responds to. The war in Vietnam represents the former, World War II the latter.

The former, largely because of its results, is regarded as embarrassing and even shameful, the latter is extolled as "the Good War."

Good wars inspire heroic stories; bad wars provoke a search for explanations. This book is a particularly thoughtful explanation of how emotion and ambition undermined rationality in the Iraq wars of the two George Bushs. The prose of these two authors is cool, their reasoning rigorous, and their conclusions both sobering and highly instructive.

Introduction

Two Surprises, Two Wars, Two Presidents, One Family

The Analytical Problem

On August 1, 1990, Iraqi troops rolled into Kuwait. During the two weeks prior to the invasion, members of the U.S. intelligence community had monitored the deployment of Iraqi forces, and several of them had concluded that Saddam Hussein intended to invade Kuwait. The intelligence evaluators forwarded their analyses to the top members of George H. W. Bush's administration, who refused to validate the conclusions until just a few hours before the start of the invasion. For the next few days, Bush and his senior advisers met to discuss Iraq's action and the manner in which the United States should respond. Prior to the second meeting, however, the president and his national security adviser had agreed that the United States could not tolerate Iraq's belligerent act and should use military force, if necessary, to expel the invaders. In view of their decision, the other senior advisers had no choice but to concur. Some time later, while the Pentagon was in the process of devising its military strategy, the senior foreign policy-makers in the Bush administration hastily decided that they would confine the operation to the extraction of the Iraqi forces from Kuwait and would refrain from marching toward Baghdad with the intent of overthrowing Saddam Hussein's regime.

In 2001, a second member of the Bush family was encumbered by a conspicuously more costly surprise attack. On September 11, three planes flown by al Qaeda operatives crashed against three major U.S.

buildings—two in New York and one in Washington.[1] Within the span of a few days, President George W. Bush ordered preparations for an attack on Afghanistan. In November, after learning that the United States and its allies had nearly succeeded at forcing the Taliban regime and al Qaeda members to abandon their strongholds in Afghanistan, the president directed Secretary of Defense Donald Rumsfeld to design a plan to topple Saddam Hussein's regime. Some 16 months later, Bush authorized the invasion of Iraq.

Rationality and Foreign Policy-Making

Foreign policy-making is about choices. World War II convinced Hans Morgenthau that its horrendous costs could have been curbed had the United States, Britain, and France acted earlier to block Germany's hegemonic aspirations. As a result, he proposed that in order to avoid repeating the same mistake foreign policy-makers must act rationally.[2] Since then, students of international politics have viewed rationality as the cornerstone of foreign policy-making. They concede that the practice of rationality does not guarantee the design of a successful policy; but they also contend that its recurrent absence eventually generates costly results to the entity the foreign policy-formulators are assigned to represent and protect.

Our analysis is steered by a set of interrelated interests. Our leading goal is to build a theoretical construct that captures the nature of the decision-making processes of the two Bush administrations. To achieve this objective we explicate and compare the way the two Bush administrations addressed the Gulf and Iraqi crises. As part of the analysis, we assess whether each administration deviated from the rational process during the crises, and if they did, we single out the factors that affected the procedures. Though originally we also intended to analyze the Afghan case, we soon realized that the policy initiated by the second Bush administration during the days preceding the attack on Afghanistan could best be explained by a simpler approach to the study of foreign policy.

The study of a president's foreign policy-making process is vital when the international problem he and his principal advisers addressed could have been dealt with differently by another group of decision-makers. The September 11 attacks on the United States left Bush and his senior advisers very little room to maneuver. Even if a different administration had led the United States at that time, it is inconceivable to think that it would not have responded with an act of war against Afghanistan had its regime refused to acquiesce to Washington's demands. As explained by realists, an act of war against any actor, but particularly against the most powerful entity in the world, forces its leaders to respond in form. Failure to do so would undermine its prestige and, possibly, its relative power.[3] The most one could conjecture at this stage is that a president other than George W. Bush, surrounded by a different group of advisers, might have opted for a different war plan. Quite possibly, a different president might not have been so driven by the conviction that he needed to respond immediately, or might have been advised by a secretary of defense who would have used a different plan of attack. Such distinctions, although important, are not pertinent to our investigation.

To help realize the previously identified analytical goals, our work focuses on the following questions:

1. Did George H. W. Bush and his senior foreign policy advisers have sufficient information to deduce that an attack on Kuwait by Iraqi forces was highly probable? If they did not, why not? If they did, what compelled them to ignore the threat?

2. Did George W. Bush and his senior foreign policy advisers have the necessary information to infer that a direct attack on U.S. soil by al Qaeda operatives was highly likely? If they did not, why not? If they did, what impelled them to disregard the warnings?

3. Did George H. W. Bush and his senior foreign policy advisers study thoroughly the problems generated by the Iraqi invasion of Kuwait? What options did they assess before deciding on the

use of military force against Iraq? What induced the president
to resort to military force to drive Iraq out of Kuwait?
4. Did George H. W. Bush and his advisers assess carefully
   whether or not to try to overthrow the Saddam Hussein regime
   in Iraq? What convinced the president not to try to overturn
   the Iraqi regime?
5. Did George W. Bush and his senior foreign policy advisers
   study meticulously the problems caused by the Saddam
   Hussein regime? What choices did they consider before deciding on the use of military force against the Saddam Hussein
   regime? What propelled the president to resort to military
   force to topple the Iraqi regime?
6. Did George W. Bush and his advisers analyze scrupulously the
   viability of instituting a democratic regime in Iraq? What
   convinced the president that it would be feasible to set up a
   democratic regime in Iraq?

Structure of the Book

To answer the questions mentioned earlier, assess whether the Bush
administrations approached their respective foreign policy-making
processes rationally, and offer a theoretical explanation for their decisions, we have divided the book into six parts. In chapter one we
conduct a brief tour of the main foreign policy-making theories thus
far devised, but refrain from positing our own. We favored this path
because we concluded that it would be markedly more helpful to
allow the data to speak for itself instead of imposing on it a precon-
ceived construct.

In chapter two, we describe the information each administration
examined prior to the surprise attacks, as well as some of the conclusions different members derived. In the case of the first Bush administration we focus also on the negotiations and discussions some of
its leading members carried on with Saddam Hussein and several
other Middle Eastern leaders during the period prior to the invasion.
In chapter three we analyze the logic behind strategies of surprise,

consider the measures the potential victim must take in order to avoid becoming an actual victim, and determine whether either Bush administration could have averted being surprised. We conclude that the first Bush administration had the information necessary to infer that Saddam Hussein intended to invade Kuwait, that several intelligence analysts alerted leading members of the administration that an attack was highly probable, and that responsibility for refusing to heed the warnings fell squarely on the shoulders of the Bush administration's central figures. We also explain why those same leaders were disinclined to take note of the warnings.

In our analysis of the second Bush administration and its inability to prevent the September 11 surprise attacks, we concur with some of the conclusions arrived at by *The 9/11 Commission Report*. It is difficult to contend, without the aid of hindsight, that had those responsible for tracking the activities of the potential terrorists been more competent, they would have been able to forewarn the senior members of the Bush administration in a timely manner and, consequently, that the attacks would have been averted. It is fair to note, however, that the intelligence gatherers failed to share information, conduct insightful and imaginative analyses, and initiate useful counterterrorist operations, and that their errors magnified the would-be surprisers' opportunity to succeed. The opportunities to the would-be surprisers were further augmented by the refusal on the part of the Bush administration's senior members to identify al Qaeda "as a first order threat" in their original foreign policy agenda.

We start chapter four with an examination of the first Bush administration's two decisions—to rely on force to free Kuwait from Iraq and to refrain from marching toward Baghdad in order to topple the Iraqi regime. In the next section, we scrutinize George W. Bush's decisions to go to war against Iraq and to replace its leadership with a democratic regime. In chapter five we conduct a detailed investigation of the decisions formulated by both administrations. Our analysis of the first Bush administration does not generate a simple conclusion. We contend that from early on President Bush and his national security adviser, Brent Scowcroft, defined the nature of the problem, the goals the United States would pursue, and the policy it would implement, with very little input from the other senior foreign policy-makers. More to the point, we argue that the decision-making process was void of any traces of rationality. It was dictated mainly by the president's deep anger against Saddam Hussein and instinctive fear of repeating the mistakes committed by France, Britain, and the United States when they refused to respond aggressively to Adolf Hitler's expansionist strategy in the 1930s. The absence of a systematic analysis was balanced by the president's decision to authorize the military to use whatever means it needed in order to bring about victory at minimal cost to the United States. In the examination of the first Bush administration's decision not to try to topple Saddam Hussein's regime, we argue that it was the result of a process generated by the belief that no one in Washington knew the kind of political system that would replace the Saddam Hussein regime, that any attempt to create a pro-U.S. government would spawn very high costs and would require extensive U.S. involvement for a lengthy period, and that it would alienate the leaders of those states who had helped in the fight against Iraq.

With respect to the second Bush administration, we postulate that it decided on war against Iraq knowing that the intelligence it possessed about Saddam Hussein's intentions and actions was inconclusive, and that it refused to give serious thought to other alternatives and to the various obstacles it would encounter in its drive to transform Iraq into a democratic state. This case demonstrates the extent to which an administration is prepared to ignore information that disputes, or casts doubt on, the rationale of its political agenda if its president demands immediate action, is deeply confident of his ideology and "gut feeling," and disparages disciplined thinking.

In chapter six we configure the various conclusions in the form of a general theoretical construct. The maxim "the apple never falls far from the tree" is partially applicable to this study. Many of the traits revealed by Bush senior during his handling of the Gulf crisis reemerged during his son's preparation for the war against Iraq.

Each president, rather than engaging in a systematic comparison of viable options, relied on his instinct when formulating the decision, and used moral language to justify his choice. Compelled to ensure that no one questioned his personal courage and motivation to "do the right thing," each leader also refused to reconsider his original decision. Both administrations used historical analogies as part of their decision-making process. The Munich fiasco and the 1989–1990 Panama crisis informed the decisions by the first President Bush. The human costs absorbed by the U.S. military in Vietnam and Lebanon dictated the strategy opted by his military advisers at the Pentagon. Two historical cases influenced the second president's decision-making process. The September 11 tragedy convinced him that permitting Saddam Hussein to remain in power was an unacceptable risk. In addition, the United States's success at transforming Germany and Japan into stable and friendly democracies led him to believe that he could replicate the task in Iraq. For many of his advisers, Saddam Hussein's deceptive behavior during the 1990s validated the use of military force against him and his regime. A few linked the Iraqi's leader behavior to Adolf Hitler's policies in the mid-1930s and the refusal on the part the United States, Great Britain, and France to counter forcefully straight away.

The effects of organizational and psychological impediments to rational foreign policy-making are captured by the "noncompensatory" decision-making theory. The construct postulates that foreign policy-makers, instead of comparing both the positive and negative aspects of a number of viable options, stress the positive factor of its favored policy and the negative elements of other alternatives. The theory is successful at encapsulating the approach to foreign policy-making by the two Bush administrations.

CHAPTER ONE
ALTERNATIVE THEORIES OF FOREIGN POLICY-MAKING

For a time students of foreign policy assumed that some ethereal overarching goal, such as the pursuit of "power" or "security," shaped the actions of states in the world arena. It remains quite common to view the single state as a conglomerate that operates as a single unit, with one central purpose across a widespread range of political activities. Although realism—the principal theory that adheres to this perspective—has substantial merit, one of its fundamental deficiencies lies in its inability to account for disparities in responses by different leaders within the same state to similar international problems. This study is built on the premise that it is not always possible to establish a priori the way state leaders will define a particular international problem, the goals they will strive to fulfill, the policies they will design, and the commands they will issue in order to attain them. This idea dictates making the process of foreign policy-crafting the focus of our analysis.

Early attempts to infuse explanations of U.S. foreign policy-making with a theoretical perspective were dominated by the assumption that decision-makers are rational in defining problems and generating policies to resolve them. With Hans Morgenthau's contention that to "search for the clue of foreign policy exclusively in the motives of statesmen is both futile and deceptive"[1] as their mantra, and the traditional microeconomic model of rational choice as their foundation, analysts sought to explicate a wide range of foreign policies designed and implemented by a variety of U.S. administrations.

Two scholars have proposed that the strategies leaders choose are a function of "the values they attach to alternative outcomes and the beliefs they hold regarding how their adversary will respond to their strategic decisions."[2] In other words, decisions are the result of a process whereby decision-makers evaluate the costs and benefits they link to each alternative and then choose that which, in their estimation, will bring about "the largest net gain (expected utility) at an acceptable level of risk."[3]

Some of these analysts, however, seem to have lost sight of the fact that Morgenthau, aware that foreign policy was rarely the result of a rational process, was not attempting to create an explanatory theory, but instead was trying to advise leaders on how they should reason. This study's second critical principle is that since rationality is an ideal, and thus unrealizable, the analysis of foreign policy-making calls for the identification of the principal obstructions to rationality and an account of the way they hinder it. This perspective can then be used to design a theoretical explanation of the way foreign policies are generated.

Impediments to Rationality

A rational response to an international problem entails proceeding along several paths, sometimes simultaneously. First, decision-makers must define the nature of the problem and determine its significance. To perform these tasks, they must have access to reliable, though not necessarily complete, information, and identify the interests at stake and their linkages. Then they must isolate a set of pertinent goals, rank them, and ascertain the extent to which they either correspond or conflict with one another. The next three endeavors involve setting apart a number of viable alternatives, weighing them against one another by including the risks they are likely to encounter in their implementation, and selecting the one with the highest expected utility. Because the resolution of an international problem often requires the execution of a series of measures throughout an extended period, decision-makers must always be prepared to evaluate the effects of the original policy and recommence the process if it falls short of realizing the initial goals or generates costly, unexpected consequences.

Hurdles to rationality in foreign policy-making have three distinct, but interconnected, sources—the intelligence agencies and the manner in which they interact with one another and the main decision-making body, the central decision-making group, and the individual decision-makers. As the world's leading actor, the United States is incessantly gathering information about potential, developing, or existing threats to its interests, both domestic and international. U.S. intelligence agencies, such as the Central Intelligence Agency (CIA), the Federal Bureau of Investigation (FBI), and the Defense Intelligence Agency (DIA) are some of the organizations responsible for this task.

Every day each intelligence agency is compelled to prioritize and compress a massive volume of information before it transmits it in the form of an intelligence briefing to the central decision-making body. The intelligence briefing is not always an accurate reflection of the information assessed by the intelligence agency. Analysts often engage in uncertainty and inconsistency absorption—that is, they exclude from their intelligence report the fact that they relied on incomplete and contradictory information to derive their inferences.[4] Sometimes their decisions to leave out uncertainties and inconsistencies are shaped by their own priorities, at other times by their reading of what the principal foreign policy-making group expects. But whatever the rationale, the actions threaten to undermine the decision-makers' ability to adequately appraise the situation.

Historically, intelligence agencies have been protective of their respective bureaucratic dominions and have sought to weaken each other's capability and reputation. The measures they have designed to undermine one another have taken different forms. It is not uncommon for an intelligence agency to approach an international problem with its own set of distinct interests in mind. When producing intelligence analyses, for instance, analysts may exaggerate the benefits or costs of particular interpretations that selectively benefit their particular agency. They may choose to avoid dealing with problems that are unlikely to enhance their interests, but that might be of significant concern to others. They may decide not to pass on information to other agencies, or to botch the bureaucratic lines of communications. In short, this shared hostile predisposition toward one another too often has resulted in the production of flawed "partisan analyses."[5]

The president surrounds himself with a small number of advisers who represent governmental institutions responsible for carrying out a variety of foreign policy tasks. The advisers keep the president informed about important developments both at home and abroad; alert him about, rising, or existing threats; help him understand and define problems; suggest alternative remedies; and serve as a sounding board as he decides on a policy. A president's personality, his value system, and the type of advisory system he creates determine the power and influence of his advisers.[6]

The size, membership, and role structure of the group can affect both the policy formulation process and the quality of the policy. Of significant concern to many analysts are the effects of "groupthink." Groupthink refers to "a mode of thinking that people engage in when they are deeply involved in a cohesive in-group, when the members' striving for unanimity overrides their motivation to realistically appraise alternative courses of action."[7] A decision-making group constrained by groupthink has one or more self-appointed mind guards, rationalizes collectively, develops illusions of invulnerability and unanimity (often by pressuring internal dissenters to conform), believes in its inherent moral superiority, thinks of other groups as enemies and less competent, and tolerates only self-censorship. During instances of high stress, members of the group tend to conduct poor information searches, consider only the information that confirms their beliefs and expectations, and carry out an incomplete survey of objectives and alternatives. They have a propensity to ignore the risks behind their preferred choice, fail to reappraise alternatives, and neglect to work out contingency plans.[8]

Each decision-making group is made up of individuals who independently can also wear away the rational process. The different theories presented later attempt to outline a variety of innate human shortcomings that impede this process. As Herbert Simon pointed out in the 1950s, no single human being possesses the intellectual capability or energy to assess all pertinent information, and to evaluate all relevant alternatives and their potential consequences. Human rationality, he stressed, is always bounded.[9] Other analysts soon broadened the analytical path opened by Simon. Cognitive psychologists emphasized the necessity of "extensive processing time, cognitive effort, concentration and skills" to achieve maximization. These conditions, however, are seldom fully present when state leaders face extraordinary pressure and time constraints.[10]

It is widely debated how the aforementioned limits on rational action are shaped in the minds of those attempting to formulate foreign policies in the tumultuous global arena. Attribution theory characterizes decision-makers as "naïve scientists" who often erroneously come to less-than-ideal decisions because they fail to recognize that the best way to test a hypothesis is by attempting to falsify it.[11] State leaders are essentially misguided sleuths who inadvertently tend to build theories as to what the proper course of action should be and then confirm their views by searching for evidence that backs them up. They are subrational actors not because of cognitive needs but because they are ignorant of their own intellectual inadequacies.

A related body of literature is schema theory. Its advocates opine that decision-makers resort to various cognitive shortcuts in order to ascertain the nature of a problem and the proper action. Decision-makers, according to this theory, are overwhelmed by a barrage of information and burdened by the lack of time and energy. Thus, they seek to understand the world as rapidly and as effortlessly as possible. This tendency is especially important when leaders are faced with new or novel information. In order to reduce uncertainty, actors will attempt to match new information and stimuli with past experiences and events. Psychologists refer to this response as "cognitive scripting"—employing a sequence of events that tells a story that lies embedded in the memory of the decision-maker. Information-processing theorists stress that decision-makers rely on scripts and try to identify analogies that help them deal with new situations. Particularly relevant to the study of international relations is the use of historical case studies perceived to be similar to the current challenge. Scripts come in different forms. Episodic scripts are based on the analysis of a single experience, while repeated experiences shape categorical scripts. Decision-makers remember experiences in which they or others were attempting to fulfill similar goals, and they make the structure applicable to the new situation in order to formulate a generalized plan of action. When confronted with a problem, moreover, the more familiar the decision-makers deem the issue, the more likely they are to respond by utilizing scripting in order to deal with it. Essentially, their intent is to create a "familiar problem space" they can rely on so that they can solve the problem with greater ease.[12]

A third psychological perspective characterizes humans as "consistency-seekers." It stresses that human beings are innately biased when they attempt to deal with a problem. As decision-makers they try both to deal with the issue at hand and to keep their core beliefs and values mutually consistent.[13] Human beings, contends the theory, are driven to shape an unwieldy, contradictory world into a coherent ideological construct that simplifies the nature of problems and gives concrete meaning and explanations for the seemingly random stimuli assaulting the senses.[14]

Intimately related to the nature of the central decision-making group and the way its members approach international problems and seek solutions is the role played by its leading figure—the president. Extensive and intensive focus on the president is justified by the fact that it is he who decides on the structure of the decision-making group that will function as his principal advising entity, and it is he who generally decides what foreign policy to implement. A president can have a substantial effect on the decision-making process by the way he interacts with his principal advisers and through his core personal attributes, such as his cognitions, analytical skills, and emotional resources.[15]

Only modest intellectual insight is needed to appreciate how cumbersome it is to formulate a parsimonious theory of foreign policy-making, considering the myriad of impediments decision-makers typically encounter. Nonetheless, as of late, two major attempts stand out. According to the "compensatory" strategy of decision-making, decision-makers assign values to each alternative's dimensions, develop an overall "score" for each alternative, and then select the alternative with the highest value. The driving assumption behind this approach is that though a particular alternative—for example, the use of force—may score low on the political dimension, such an alternative could still be adopted if it scored high on the military dimension.[16] Those who argue that foreign policy-makers rely on cognitive short-cuts to rational decision-making have challenged this perspective. They contend that decisions are based not on a compensatory calculus but on a noncompensatory process. Foreign policy-makers do not depend on rules "that require the evaluation and comparison of all alternatives across different dimensions . . ." Instead, they rely on a perspective that enables them to adopt or reject "alternatives on the basis of one or a few criteria."[17] For instance, when two important dimensions are present in an alternative and one is negative, the foreign policy-makers, instead of comparing the extent to which the positive dimension compensates the negative one in each alternative, typically reject any alternative that has a negative dimension.

Analytical Framework

Based on the aforementioned discussion of decision-making theories, there are a number of approaches one can use to analyze the way the two Bush administrations formulated their respective policies toward Iraq, and the extent to which each deviated from the rational process. One method would be to identify a priori one of the theories just discussed or postulate a new one, and then conduct an empirical analysis of the two administrations to test its applicability. A second option would be to impose a number of pertinent foreign policy-making theories on the two administrations in order to isolate the one that derives the best explanation. A third alternative would be to conduct a thorough empirical analysis of both cases, steered by a set of carefully designed questions, with the intent of isolating the dominant obstacles each administration faced so as to derive a theoretical construct inductively. Our analysis is shaped by the third approach.

We favor the last perspective for a number of reasons. First, as social scientists, we are too often afflicted by the yearning to be identified with a particular theoretical argument or as one of its leading designers. This urge sometimes drives us to disregard evidence that could either weaken or falsify our theoretical construct. Second, it is imprudent to assume that any one foreign policy-making theory can capture the varied responses to international problems fashioned by decision-making groups with different characteristics led by presidents with unlike attributes and qualities. Third, it is exceedingly difficult to draw a clear conceptual divide between some of the competing foreign policy-making theories; this is to say that there is substantial crossover from one theory to another. Fourth, not every theory focuses on the same types of actors. As noted earlier, some theories concentrate on the impact of bureaucratic competition between the various intelligence agencies; others try to decipher the overall effect of the main foreign-making group; while a third group ponders about the actions of the decision- making group's leading figures. An argument built inductively, though markedly less elegant than the previous options, enables analysts to isolate the different elements identified by the various theories, and to restructure them in the shape of an alternative theoretical construct.

To single out the impediments to rationality encountered or generated by each of the two administrations and explain their respective effects, we bring into play a relatively simple analytical method. Each foreign policy begins with the identification and definition of a problem. The way a problem is defined can have a decisive effect on the formulation of a foreign policy.[18] Sometimes intelligence analysts working within the same or different bureaucracies identify an event or a set of events as a problem and try to warn their superiors of its existence. At other times, members of the leading decision-making group carry out the identification. The classification of a problem is not always followed by the admission on the part of those who did not participate in the task that the supposed problem is, in fact, a problem, or by an agreement as to how it should be interpreted. Because both Bush administrations encountered these challenges, we begin with an analysis of the obstacles each one came across as some of its members sought to alert others of a mounting threat; how the leading decision-makers came to define the threat, with a special focus on the types of interests they claimed had been, or were being, affected; and what influenced their decision to define it the way they did. To describe the impediments each administration encountered and the way it addressed them, we conduct a series of interrelated procedures. We identify the information available to each administration, explain the inferences the respective intelligence analysts and the principal decision-makers derived from the available information, assess the extent to which the existing information backed the alternative inferences, describe the rationales posited by the leading members of each administration to validate their inferences, and put forward explanations for the proposed rationales.

As explained earlier, in a rational foreign policy-making process the leading decision-makers, after coming up with a formulation of the problem, must identify possible alternatives and gauge their suitability. In order to decide which alternative to implement, they must first appraise each goal's import, examine the problems their concurrent quest could generate, and compare the potential effectiveness of various options. An investigation of how each administration performed this portion of the process calls for a determination of whether the core decision-making group's organizational structure aided or impeded the conduct of judicious appraisals, and it calls for an explanation as to the manner in which each group's distinct characteristics helped engender either effect. It also entails assessing the extent to which the central decision-makers engaged in thoughtful evaluations of possible goals and policies. This assessment requires an examination of the evidence the decision-makers relied on to rationalize their choices, and on the identification of the cognitive and motivational factors that affected their judgments and helped determine their final choice.

CHAPTER TWO
TWO HARMFUL SURPRISES

The March Toward Kuwait

During a visit to the White House in October 1989, Iraq's foreign minister, Tariq Aziz, complained to President George H. W. Bush and Secretary of State James Baker that the United States had launched a campaign designed to embarrass and humiliate his country. Aziz was referring to accusations by the U.S. Congress and media that Iraq was developing nuclear and chemical weapons, that its banking practices were corrupt, and that its human rights record was reprehensible. Critical comments about Saddam Hussein's leadership style, added the foreign minister, further weakened the prospect of a better relationship between Iraq and the United States. He then noted that Baghdad was concerned with the U.S. Department of Agriculture's decision to reduce its agricultural credit to Iraq to $400 million. Both U.S. leaders sought to convince Aziz that the United States was determined to work with Iraq to bring peace and stability in the Middle East. In addition, Baker promised that he would try to reverse the credit decision.[1]

When criticisms emanating from the United States continued, both sides concurred it would be helpful to meet again. On February 11, 1990, Undersecretary of State for Near Eastern Affairs John Kelly spent two hours with the Iraqi leader in Baghdad. During the meeting, Saddam Hussein noted that in view of the Soviet Union's tribulations, the United States would be in a position to dominate Middle Eastern affairs for some five years, and hinted that he was prepared to work with Washington. He wondered, however, whether the Bush administration was ready to initiate a "constructive" policy or would continue to promote Israel's goals. Kelly reaffirmed Bush and Baker's earlier commitment to work with Iraq to promote stability and peace in the Middle East.[2] Later that month, Saddam Hussein voiced his apprehension publicly. In a speech broadcast on Jordanian television, the Iraqi leader claimed that because of the Soviet Union's waning power, the United States could become the Middle East's hegemon. "The country that will have the greatest influence in the region, through the Arab gulf and its oil," said Saddam Hussein, "will maintain its superiority as a superpower without an equal to compete with it. This means that if the Gulf people, along with all Arabs, are not careful, the Arab region will be governed by the wishes of the United States."[3]

At the beginning of April, Saddam Hussein became more belligerent. In a widely publicized talk, he bragged about his country's chemical weapons capability and threatened to burn half of Israel if it attacked Iraq. "[W]e will make the fire eat up half of Israel, if it tries to do anything against Iraq."[4] The Bush administration called the speech "inflammatory, irresponsible, and outrageous."[5] A few days later, the Iraqi leader asked Saudi Arabia's ruler, King Fahd, to send a trusted representative to Iraq to discuss the latest developments in the region. In a meeting with the Saudi ambassador to the United States, Amir Bandar bin Sultan, Iraq's ruler made it clear that he would not attack Israel, but that he needed a guarantee from the United States that Israel would not attack Iraq. Bandar returned to Washington and delivered Saddam Hussein's message to Bush on April 9. During his conversation with Bandar, Bush wondered why Saddam Hussein would threaten Israel if he did not plan to attack it. The meeting ended without the U.S. president's extending an assurance. Bush and Bandar met again in mid-April, at which time the president agreed to talk to the Israelis. When contacted by the White House, the Israelis made it clear that they would not attack Iraq so long as Iraq restrained itself. Saddam Hussein received Israel's pledge directly from the United States. Later in April, a group of visiting U.S. senators, led by Robert Dole, met with Saddam Hussein and reiterated Washington's earlier message. Dole presented the Iraqi leader a letter stating that the group was there to help "improve bilateral relations between our nations."[6]

Saddam Hussein's concern with Israel was warranted. He remembered 1981, when Israel launched a surprise attack that destroyed Iraq's nuclear plant. Because at that time Iraq was entrenched in a war with Iran, Baghdad did not retaliate. Thus, as he contemplated launching an attack on Kuwait in 1990, Saddam Hussein wanted to be assured that as he exposed one of his country's flanks, Israel would not be tempted to mount another destructive operation.[7] Confident that Israel would restrain itself, Saddam Hussein decided he could take action against a lesser adversary—Kuwait.

Iraq's rancor toward Kuwait had a history. For strategic and economic reasons, Iraq had not welcomed Kuwait's independence in 1961; consequently, it withheld diplomatic recognition until 1963. From that day on, Baghdad repeatedly pressed Kuwait to relinquish control of two islands and parts of an area bordering Iraq. During that same period, Iraq was forced to contend with the Shah of Iran, who disapproved of Baghdad's decision to distance itself from the West and establish a closer relationship with Moscow. The relationship between Iraq and Kuwait continued to deteriorate, even during the Iraq–Iran war.[8] When the war ended, Saddam Hussein faced a problematic future. Iran remained a formidable threat, whereas a broken oil industry, a massive foreign debt, and thousands of returning soldiers clamoring for jobs that had long vanished burdened Iraq's economy. Determined to alleviate his country's economic ills, the Iraqi leader sent one of his emissaries to Kuwait in December 1989. The envoy's task was to resolve the frontier dispute, stop the steady fall of world oil prices, and obtain from Kuwait a ten billion dollar loan for reconstruction and economic development.[9]

When Kuwait failed to respond in the manner he had demanded, the Iraqi leader increased the pressure. On May 28, 1990, during an Arab summit meeting held in Baghdad, he criticized Kuwait's overproduction and low oil prices. Iraq, noted Saddam Hussein, "is in a state of economic warfare. [S]ome Arab countries whose heads of state are present at this meeting," he explained, "have pursued a policy of oil overproduction leading to the lowering of oil prices to its lowest level . . . to Iraq, every lowering of one dollar in the price of oil has resulted in a loss of one billion dollars a year . . ."[10] Attempts by various Middle Eastern leaders to curb the growing tension between the aggrieved parties achieved little. Hence, on July 15 and 16, Baghdad exerted additional pressure. On the first day, Iraq's foreign minister sent a memorandum to the Arab League accusing Kuwait of pursuing "a policy that hurt Iraq . . ." He claimed that Baghdad had attempted to resolve the frontier differences peacefully, and had asked Kuwait to reduce its oil production and cancel Iraq's ten billion dollar debt.[11] The following day, Saddam Hussein went on television to denounce both Kuwait and the United Arab Emirates for exceeding their oil production quotas, as set by the Organization of Petroleum Exporting Countries (OPEC). Their action, he explained, caused the price of oil to plummet from $18 to $7 a barrel and cost Iraq billions of dollars in lost revenue. To ensure that Kuwait would not take his denunciation lightly, and to measure how Washington would respond to an aggressive act against Kuwait, Saddam Hussein deployed a brigade of one of his country's most powerful tank divisions close to Kuwait's northern border and ordered the loading of equipment belonging to the Republican Guard on trains.

The Bush administration and its intelligence analysts did not ignore Saddam Hussein's belligerent actions. Walter P. Lang, the Pentagon's senior civilian intelligence analyst for the Middle East and South Asia Region, noticed, as he studied the latest satellite photos, both the brigade of tank divisions that Iraq had deployed close to Kuwait's northern border and the loading of trains with equipment belonging to the Republican Guard.[12] This development, Lang feared, could thwart President Bush's push to strengthen the United States's relationship with Iraq, which had been outlined in his October 2, 1989, National Security Directive 26. The "United States Government should propose economic and political incentives for Iraq to moderate its behavior and to increase our influence with Iraq."[13] Still, Lang knew that he did not have enough information to deduce what Saddam Hussein intended to do with his newly deployed forces.

Lang was not the only one troubled by Saddam Hussein's actions. National Security Adviser Brent Scowcroft, in particular, wondered about Saddam Hussein's "abrupt change" in behavior. He feared that the change made it difficult for the United States to predict what the Iraqi leader intended to do next.[14] In the meantime, Secretary of Defense Dick Cheney cautioned Iraq that the Bush administration would "take seriously any threats to U.S. interests or U.S. friends in the region."[15]

The secretary of defense's warning did not deter Saddam Hussein. By July 19, he had deployed three of Iraq's tank divisions and some 35,000 men to within 10–30 miles of the Kuwaiti border. While other foreign policy problems compelled Scowcroft to redirect his attention, Lang remained alert. After noticing the latest Iraqi troop movement, Lang wrote a report to Lieutenant General Harry E. Soyster, his superior and director of the DIA, in which he stated that whatever Saddam Hussein was preparing, it was "not a rehearsal." Lang described the troop movement and presaged that it was typical of Saddam Hussein to conduct operations and battles in vacant areas before engaging Iraqi tanks. At this stage, however, the intelligence analyst was not prepared to conclude that the Iraqi leader would order his troops to march into Kuwait. On that same day, the U.S. Department of Defense sent mixed signals. Cheney reaffirmed the United States's commitment to help Kuwait defend itself were it to be attacked. Later on, however, a Pentagon spokesperson qualified the secretary's statement by saying that the press had quoted him "with some degree of liberty."[16]

Lang's report had little effect. A Department of Defense intelligence digest circulated the following day left out his assessment and speculated that Iraq "was unlikely to use significant force against Kuwait . . ."[17] The chairman of the Joint Chiefs of Staff, though troubled by Iraq's actions, was not alarmed. General Colin Powell noted that Iraq had not completed many of the steps typically taken by a state getting ready to launch an attack, such as augmenting the communications network in the area, putting in place artillery stocks and other munitions necessary for offensive action, and increasing the supply line.[18] The Joint Chiefs of Staff's director of operations, Lieutenant General Thomas W. Kelly, also remained confident that Saddam Hussein would not resort to extreme measures. Kelly speculated that the Iraqi leader was merely attempting to pressure Kuwait to acquiesce to his demands, and that he might take an oil field or the two small islands in the Persian Gulf that Iraq had been wanting to control for quite some time. General H. Norman Schwarzkopf, who as commander of the Central Command was responsible for overseeing U.S. military interests in the Middle East and Southwest Asia, agreed with his colleagues' assessments. He thought that Iraq at most would launch a punitive but limited attack against Kuwait. Top officials at the White House and Department of State also showed limited concern. And the CIA argued that it would be unprecedented for one Arab state to attack another. In short, most senior officials in the Bush administration clung to the argument that Iraq was simply practicing the "1990 equivalent of gunboat diplomacy."[19]

During the next few days, the Bush administration continued to forward conflicting signals. When the CIA reported that Iraq had deployed some of its troops near the Kuwaiti border, the Department of Defense sent two KC-135 tankers and a C-141 cargo transport to the Gulf to participate in joint exercises with the United Arab Emirates. It also moved six warships closer to Kuwait to, in the words of a Pentagon official, "lay down a marker for Saddam Hussein." The secretary of the navy attempted to reinforce the message by noting during a House Armed Services Subcommittee that U.S. "ships in the Persian Gulf were put on full alert." Shortly afterward, however, a Pentagon spokesperson stated that the secretary's statement was erroneous. A few days later, a Department of State spokesperson explained that the United States did "not have any defense treaties with Kuwait, and there are no special defense or security commitments to Kuwait." That same day, a Pentagon official remarked that the United States remained "strongly committed to supporting the individual and collective self-defense of [its] friends in the Gulf . . ."

When asked whether the United States would help Kuwait if it were attacked, he did not answer.[20]

In the meantime, Saddam Hussein continued to gauge the United States's commitment to protect Kuwait. On July 25 he met with April Glaspie, the U.S. ambassador to Iraq. The Iraqi leader started the meeting by emphasizing the need for mutual understanding, and then stated that he wanted his conversation with her to be a "message to President Bush."[21] He noted that when the interests between two countries "are limited and relations are not old, then there isn't a deep understanding and mistakes could have a negative effect. Sometimes the effect of an error can be larger than the error itself." He also tried to explain his concern about the drop in the price of oil. "[W]hen planned and deliberate policy forces the price of oil down without good commercial reasons, then that means another war against Iraq . . . Kuwait and the UAE were at the front of this policy aimed at lowering Iraq's position and depriving its people of higher economic standards." He then added that the United States had to "have a better understanding of the situation and declare who it wants to have relations with and who its enemies are."[22]

The U.S. ambassador responded by stating that the Bush administration hoped to find a way to improve the relationship between the United States and Iraq. April Glaspie explained that she had "direct instruction from the President to seek better relations with Iraq," and apologized for how some members of the U.S. media had depicted the Iraqi leader.[23] Afterward she asked Saddam Hussein to explain what he hoped to achieve by deploying his forces so close to the Kuwaiti border. "[W]e can only see that you have deployed massive troops in the south. Normally that would not be any of our business. But when this happens in the context of what you said on your national day, then when we read the details in the two letters of the foreign minister, then when we see the Iraqi point of view that the measures taken by the UAE and Kuwait is, in the final analysis, parallel to military aggression against Iraq, then it would be reasonable for me to be concerned. And for this reason, I received an instruction to ask you, in the spirit of friendship—not in the spirit of confrontation—regarding your intentions."[24] Saddam Hussein's response was succinct. After stating that he understood the United States's concern, he reiterated that he wanted "others to know that [Iraq's] patience [was] running out regarding their action," and that although Iraq was not an aggressor, it did not "accept aggression either." He added that he had no intention of doing "anything until we meet with them [the Kuwaitis]. When we meet and we see that there is hope, then nothing will happen. But if we are unable to find a solution, then it will be natural that Iraq will not accept death, even though wisdom is above everything else." Convinced that Saddam Hussein wanted a peaceful solution to the problem, Ambassador Glaspie left for Washington soon after.

To underscore that he had no intention of acting rashly, Saddam Hussein ensured that other Middle Eastern leaders and his own ambassador to the United States would convey the same message to Washington. During a meeting with President Hosni Mubarak of Egypt, the Iraqi leader emphasized that so "long as discussions last between Iraq and Kuwait, I won't use force. I won't intervene with force before I have exhausted all the possibilities for negotiation."[25] Mubarak relayed the information to Richard Haass, the National Security Council (NSC) director for Near East and South Asian Affairs. The Egyptian president told Haass that Saddam Hussein had said, "I am not going to do it." Mubarak then added that the Iraqi military buildup was little more than "posturing."[26] King Hussein of Jordan conveyed a similar message to the U.S. president and to the chairman of the Joint Chief of Staff.[27] During this same period, the Iraqi ambassador to the United States, Muhammad al-Mashat, told John Kelly that Iraq was "not going to move against anybody."[28]

Bush and his senior foreign policy advisers welcomed the reassuring messages. He and Scowcroft, despite the fact that they had not read the ambassador's report, were encouraged by what others had told them. The president, in particular, felt that the "political crisis" had "eased."[29] More importantly, Bush, Scowcroft, and Powell, convinced that almost no one in Washington "knew the internal situation in Iraq nor Saddam Hussein," concluded that their "best bet was to take counsel from the people who did know him and who did deal with him."[30] Not only did they believe Mubarak when he told them that Saddam Hussein was merely posturing and that the crisis was like a "summer cloud" which would soon be blown away by fairer winds, but they also accepted King Hussein's contention that the feeling in the Middle East was that Saddam Hussein was deploying his forces to compel Kuwait to accept his demands.[31]

Recent history also affected the way Bush and his senior advisers estimated Saddam Hussein's intentions. By the end of its war with Iran, Iraq faced a ruined economy, an acute foreign debt, and thousands of unemployed demobilized soldiers. These conditions, reasoned Washington's top foreign policy officials, placed a straightjacket on Saddam Hussein's ability to initiate, in the coming years, any new endeavor that might shake up the region. Coincidentally, a Defense Special Assessment (DSA) concluded on July 25 that Iraq was "using rhetoric, diplomatic pressure, and significant military posturing to force Kuwait to comply with recent oil and economic demands. Although unlikely to use military pressure, Iraq [was] marshalling forces sufficient to invade Kuwait. With forces currently in place, Iraq would be able to overwhelm Kuwaiti forces and likely occupy its limited objectives within 48 hours, or all of Kuwait in five days."[32]

Many U.S. intelligence analysts did not share their bosses' hopes. By July 30, Lang no longer doubted Saddam Hussein's intention. After reevaluating the data and reassessing what he knew about the Iraqi leader, he warned General Soyster that Saddam Hussein had "created the capability to overrun all of Kuwait and all of Eastern Saudi Arabia." "If he attacks," continued Lang, "given his disposition, we will have no warning. I do not believe he is bluffing. I have looked at his personality profile. He doesn't know how to bluff. It is not in his pattern of behavior. I fear that Kuwait will be so stiff-necked in answering his demands that they will not fulfill his minimal requirements. In short, Saddam Hussein has moved a force disproportionate to the task at hand, [and] if it is to bluff then there is only one answer: he intends to use it."[33] Soyster still disagreed with Lang's analysis, but he submitted it to Cheney and Powell as part of a Defense Intelligence Digest. In the report, the Pentagon's intelligence director wrote: "Saddam Hussein will probably maintain Iraq's military stance until Kuwait agrees to his demands. Some military action is likely if Kuwait is resolute."[34] Neither the secretary of defense nor the chairman of the Joint Chiefs of Staff was prepared to consider the possibility that Saddam Hussein was about to invade Kuwait. Ironically, during this period, a number of nongovernmental organizations, with significantly fewer resources than the Pentagon, suspected that Saddam Hussein was preparing to launch an attack on Kuwait. For instance, on July 21, 1990, less than two weeks before the attack, *The Economist* wrote that the latest steps taken by Iraq sounded "alarmingly like a pretext for invasion."[35]

In the meantime, the CIA still seemed unable to decipher what Saddam Hussein intended to do. In a report to the White House, it concluded that starting a ground war in temperatures around 108 degrees Fahrenheit would be unwise, making an invasion of Kuwait highly unlikely. But, as in the DIA, there were those who dissented from the institution's official conclusions. Charlie Allen, the CIA's national warning officer, shared Lang's apprehension, but for a different reason. The latest CIA surveillance reports had shown that Iraq's forces were operating under EMCON conditions (short for Emission Control, also known as radio silence). This meant that the Iraqis, in an effort to conceal their movements and locations, were not using any radio transmissions.[36] Allen's new information was passed on to Under Secretary of State for Political Affairs Robert Kimmitt, who decided it would be wise to call for a meeting of the Deputies Committee. Allen's analysis did not alter the attendees' opinion. Dick Kerr, the CIA's deputy director, opined that an Iraqi invasion of Kuwait was virtually impossible, and though Kimmitt and Haass expressed concern, both were reluctant to challenge the status quo in light of Glaspie's wire. By the end of the meeting, the group agreed that Secretary of State Baker should send a message to Saddam Hussein proposing that Baghdad reciprocate Washington's desire for improved relations.[37]

Saddam Hussein continued to deploy his forces. By August 1, U.S. satellite photographs showed that Iraq's three armored divisions had been moved to within three miles of the Kuwaiti border, with two positioned close to the main four-lane highway leading into the center of Kuwait, and the third standing on its western side. Artillery units, which Iraq would need in order to initiate an offensive ground maneuver, were also deployed along the Kuwaiti border and were fully operational. For Lang the latest deployment signaled only one thing—an Iraqi attack was imminent. This time the CIA concurred—it warned that all indicators pointed to an impending invasion. In a separate meeting at the Department of Defense, its top officials, including Powell and Cheney, concluded that Saddam Hussein "would not invade."[38] Powell acknowledged that it was difficult to disregard the latest data, but then noted that because Iraq was ruled by a totalitarian regime and the United States lacked good human sources inside the government, which could assess Saddam Hussein's intentions, it was still too early to conclude that he planned to attack. Saddam Hussein's behavior, explained Powell "looked like bluster, it looked like an armed threat really for the purpose of achieving some diplomatic or political objective, but it didn't look like an invasion . . ."[39] The chairman of the Joint Chiefs of Staff, moreover, could not understand why Saddam Hussein would use some 100,000 troops if he planned to invade Kuwait, when he could achieve the same objective with far fewer forces. Cheney shared Powell's skepticism. He argued that there was no way to determine whether the Iraqi leader was planning to go to war or was merely attempting to scare the Kuwaitis. His analysis was almost a replica of the briefing he and the Joint Chiefs had received from Schwarzkopf.

The mood changed considerably later in the day. After reviewing additional satellite photos, the DIA confirmed that Iraqi artillery units, required for any sort of offensive ground maneuver, had become fully operational and mobilized along the Kuwaiti border. Alarmed by the news, Haass made it the primary item on that day's Deputies' Committee meeting. The conference lasted until around 5:00 p.m. By the time it ended, those attending had agreed that Iraq was likely to do "something" and that President Bush should call its ruler to warn him not to invade Kuwait.[40]

Haass phoned Scowcroft as soon as the meeting was over. He convinced his boss to organize an impromptu private talk with the president. Bush was in the White House Medical Office getting a deep-heat treatment for his shoulder when the two advisers arrived at 8:20 p.m. Bush knew the likely purpose of the unscheduled gathering, but that evening his mind "was on things other than Iraq."[41] It would only be a matter of moments for Iraq to quickly reemerge on his radar. "Mr. President," stated Scowcroft, "it looks very bad. Iraq may be about to invade Kuwait." Bush remained composed, but he was surprised. He was aware of reports of "new military activity" but had not been disturbed by them because intelligence analysts "could not confirm anything more definitive about Iraqi intentions than the movements themselves."[42] Following Scowcroft's general comments, Haass delved into some of the specific intelligence that alluded to an imminent Iraqi military attack. He then advanced the Deputies Committee's opinion that the president should contact Saddam Hussein personally and attempt to convince him not to take military action. There were two logistical problems with that plan, however. By then it was already well into the middle of the night in Baghdad. Furthermore, it was unprecedented for Bush to simply place a call to Saddam Hussein. Communication between the two leaders had been conducted through each state's respective foreign minister and ambassador. Nevertheless, the president agreed to set protocol aside. But just when he reached for the phone to try to contact Saddam Hussein, Scowcroft received a phone call. It was Kimmitt, calling to inform him that the U.S. embassy in Kuwait was reporting gunfire in downtown Kuwait. "So much for calling Saddam Hussein," shrugged Bush, as he put the phone back in its cradle. Next morning, the DIA confirmed that Iraqi forces had driven all the way to the Kuwaiti–Saudi-Arabian border.[43] By then, the U.S. president had no choice but to accept the fact that though he and his advisers had the most sophisticated intelligence system in the world at their disposal and had gathered enough information to infer that Saddam Hussein might invade Kuwait, they were surprised by his action.

A Second, More Costly Surprise

In January 2001, a new group of decision-makers assumed control of the executive branch in Washington. Most of its leading figures were hardly new to the scene. Condoleezza Rice, George W. Bush's national security adviser, had served as a NSC staffer during the Cold War's closing days. Rice's deputy Stephen Hadley had worked as assistant secretary of defense for international security affairs during the first Bush administration. Cheney, who had played major roles in three previous administrations, including that of secretary of defense for the new president's father, was now vice president. Powell, after serving as national security adviser for Reagan, and then as chairman of the Joint Chiefs of Staff in the first Bush administration, assumed the role of secretary of state. Richard Armitage, who became Powell's deputy, had worked under the Reagan administration as assistant secretary of defense for international security affairs. Secretary of Defense Donald Rumsfeld had held the same post during the latter half of Gerald Ford's short-lived presidency. And his deputy Paul Wolfowitz had worked for Cheney at the Department of Defense as under secretary of defense for policy. The only major political figure who had never served in Washington was the president himself.

The leading members of the new administration assumed their roles convinced that power competition between major states remained the leading definer of world politics. In this kind of system, the United States had to take advantage of its special status. For the president and his national security adviser, this meant that its military had to be sufficiently powerful to "deter war, project power, and fight in defense of its interests if deterrence fails . . ." and had to be able to stop "the emergence of any hostile military power in the Asia-Pacific region, the Middle East, the Persian Gulf, and Europe—areas in which not only our interests but also those of our key allies are at stake." Specifically, Washington had to deal with China not as a "status quo" power but as one that wanted to alter in its favor Asia's power distribution. It had "to mobilize whatever resources it" could to help remove Saddam Hussein from power so that Iraq would not develop weapons of mass destruction (WMD); it had to enforce its policy of deterrence against North Korea in a resolute and decisive manner; and it had to prevent Iran from spreading fundamentalist Islam throughout the international system.[44]

This world vision did not harmonize with that of the departing administration. It was the retiring president who first cautioned the newly elected president that his administration might need to reassess its global perspective. During a two-hour, one-on-one discussion of national security and foreign policy issues in December 2000, President William Clinton said to the incoming president: "I think you will find that by far your biggest threat is bin Laden and al Qaeda."[45] Bush received a similar warning from CIA director George Tenet just a few days before he was sworn in as president. In front of Bush, who was accompanied by Cheney and Rice, Tenet and his deputy for operations, James L. Pavitt, warned that the United States faced three major challenges: (i) Osama bin Laden and his al Qaeda network, (ii) the increasing proliferation of WMD, and (iii) the rise of China's military power. The last threat, however, was 5–15 years away.[46]

Richard Clarke, the national coordinator for security, infrastructure protection, and counterterrorism, delivered the third early warning. During the Clinton administration, Clarke had chaired the Counterterrorism Security Group (CSG), an assembly of specialists within the NSC. Clarke, who was one of the few high-ranking bureaucrats to be retained from the old administration, spent much of the month of January bringing his new bosses and colleagues up-to-date on the current terrorist threats to the United States. In meetings with Cheney, Powell, Rice, and Hadley, Clarke drew a stark picture. "Al Qaeda," he explained, "is at war with [the United States], it is a highly capable organization, probably with sleeper cells in the U.S., and it is clearly planning a major series of attacks against [the United States]; we must act decisively and quickly, deciding on the issues prepared after the attack on the *Cole*, going on the offensive."[47] On January 25, Clarke wrote a memorandum to Rice in which he repeated part of his earlier warning. Al Qaeda, he stated, "is not some narrow little terrorist issue that needs to be included in broader regional policy. Rather, several of our regional policies need to address centrally the transnational challenge to the U.S. and our interests posed by [al Qaeda] network." Al Qaeda, added Clarke, is "using a distorted version of Islam as its vehicle to achieve two goals: (i) to drive the U.S. out of the Muslim world, forcing the withdrawal of our military and economic presence in countries from Morocco to Indonesia; (ii) to replace moderate, modern, Western regime in Muslim countries with theocracies modeled along the lines of the Taliban."[48]

There are three ways of gauging the value placed by an administration on any one particular issue. The most straightforward manner is to focus on the kinds of discussions carried out by the principal foreign policy-makers. One can also derive valuable inferences by analyzing who the specialists report to and the amount of funding allocated to address a problem. Despite the fact that in January Clarke had asked Rice to meet with the Principals Committee in order to persuade its members that they should give terrorism a very high priority, the committee did not meet to address the challenges posed by al Qaeda until seven days before the fateful attacks on the United States.[49] It was the national security adviser who, indirectly, ensured that the meeting would not be held until such a late date.

In the previous administration, the president's national security adviser, Sandy Berger, had authorized the CSG to serve parallel to the Deputies Committee. This organizational structure enabled Clarke to report directly to the principals. Rice altered it and informed Clarke that thereafter he would report to the Deputies Committee. The effect of this change was to slow down the decision-making process. The Deputies Committee met in early March to discuss Clarke's various proposals but did not forward any type of recommendation. The next major gathering took place on the last day of April. At the meeting, the CIA representative described al Qaeda as "the most dangerous group we face" and warned that it would launch "more attacks."[50] Clarke, in turn, recommended that the Bush administration "put pressure on both the Taliban and al Qaeda by arming the Northern Alliance and other groups in Afghanistan." He also suggested that the United States target "bin Laden and his leadership by reinstating flights of the Predator." Wolfowitz challenged Clarke by wondering why anyone would be so worried "about this one man bin Laden" instead of focusing on "Iraqi terrorism." Two of the participants came to Clarke's defense. John McLaughlin, the CIA's deputy director, emphasized that his agency had "no evidence of any active terrorist threat against the U.S." by Iraq, while Armitage stated unequivocally that the Department of State saw "al Qaeda as a major threat and countering it as an urgent priority."[51] By the end of the meeting, the involved parties had agreed to initiate a comprehensive review of U.S. policy toward Pakistan and to explore the idea of supporting regime change in Afghanistan.

Little of great importance ensued until May 29, when Rice, at Tenet's behest, decided to convert their weekly meeting into a discussion on al Qaeda. Clarke and several other counterterrorist experts were invited to attend. The meeting proved to be critical. The national security adviser finally acknowledged that a set of options for attacking bin Laden had to be developed, and asked Clarke to take the lead. In early June, Rice's deputy circulated the first draft— one that called for the elimination of the al Qaeda network. By September, the Deputies Committee had designed a presidential directive that called for a three-stage strategy against Afghanistan's Taliban regime. If by the end of the second phase the United States had not persuaded the Taliban leadership to change its ways, the Bush administration would try covert action to topple the regime from within. Throughout this period, the CIA analyzed possible covert activities against the Taliban and weighed the advisability of using the Predator for reconnaissance purposes and equipping with warheads. On September 4, the Principals Committee approved the draft presidential directive with almost no discussion.[52]

To prevent acts of aggression against the state, its leaders must focus not only on ways to undermine the power of the potential assailant but also on how to prevent it from initiating an attack. The Bush administration's record on the second task was mixed. The FBI, which falls under the jurisdiction of the Department of Justice, was responsible for uncovering and preventing attacks initiated within and against the United States. Between 1995 and 2000, during a period of a decreasing federal budget, the Clinton administration increased the overall federal counterterrorism budget from $5.7 billion to $11.1 billion. During that same time, the FBI's counterterrorism budget was augmented by some 280 percent.[53] The arrival of a new attorney general brought about a major shift in priorities. On May 9, John Ashcroft noted at a congressional hearing on federal efforts to combat terrorism that one of his top priorities "would be to protect [the United States's] citizens . . . from terrorist attacks." Despite his claim, the following day the Department of Justice issued its budget guidance in which it "highlighted gun crimes, narcotics trafficking, and civil rights as priorities," but not counterterrorism. Ashcroft buttressed the Bush administration's disinclination to alter its priorities when he denied, on September 10, a request by the FBI to make its counterterrorism budget for the 2003 fiscal year larger than that for the previous period.[54]

To contend that the Bush administration was not prepared to allocate the resources requested by high-ranking bureaucrats to prevent acts of terrorism within the United States is not to argue that it was unaware a major threat loomed or that investigators were doing little to unearth al Qaeda's plans. By the start of 2001, the United States knew that Osama bin Laden and al Qaeda had been responsible for attacks in Aden, Yemen, in 1992; Mogadishu, Somalia, in 1993; Riyadh, Saudi Arabia, in 1993; Dhahran, Saudi Arabia, in 1996; Nairobi, Kenya, and Dar es Salaam, Tanzania, in 1998; and Aden, Yemen, in 2000. It also knew that bin Laden and his fighters had been based in Afghanistan since 1996.[55] By the same token, the United States had little doubt about bin Laden's intention and rationale. In the words of a long-time CIA analyst of bin Laden's activities, the al Qaeda leader had "been precise in telling America the reasons he is waging war on us. None of the reasons have anything to do with our freedom, liberty, and democracy, but everything to do with U.S. policies and actions in the Muslim world."[56] In February of 1998, operating out of a remote headquarter in Afghanistan, bin Laden prepared and faxed a declaration to the Arabic newspaper *Al-Quds al-'Arab* in London. A few days later, *Al-Quds al-'Arab* printed bin Laden's document. Bin Laden began the communiqué by calling upon all Muslims to recall and acknowledge three facts.[57]

> First, for over seven years the United States has been occupying the lands of Islam in the holiest of places, the Arabian Peninsula plundering its riches, dictating to its rulers, humiliating its people, terrorizing its neighbors, and turning its bases in the Peninsula into a spearhead through which to fight the neighboring Muslim peoples. If some people have in the past argued about the fact of the occupation, all the people of the Peninsula have now acknowledged it. The best proof of this is the Americans' continuing aggression against the Iraqi people using the Peninsula as a staging post, even though all its rulers are against their territories being used to that end, but they are helpless.
>
> Second, despite the great devastation inflicted on the Iraqi people by the crusader–Zionist alliance, and despite the huge number of those killed, which has exceeded one million . . . despite all this, the Americans are once again trying to repeat the horrific massacres, as though they are not content with the protracted blockade imposed after the ferocious war or the fragmentation and devastation. So here they come to annihilate what is left of this people and to humiliate their Muslim neighbors.
>
> Third, if the Americans' aims behind these wars are religious and economic, the aim is also to serve the Jews' petty state and divert attention from its occupation of Jerusalem and murder of Muslims there. The best proof of this is their eagerness to destroy Iraq, the strongest neighboring Arab state, and their endeavor to fragment all the states of the region such as Iraq, Saudi Arabia, Egypt, and Sudan into paper stateless and through their disunion and weakness to guarantee Israel's survival and the continuation of the brutal crusade occupation of the Peninsula.

Bin Laden closed with a declaration of war, calling for attacks against all Americans, both civilian and military.[58] He repeated al Qaeda's intention to attack inside and outside the United States, in markedly more devastating ways, after its fighters had struck the destroyer USS *Cole* in 2000.[59] None of these challenges was overlooked by U.S. intelligence.

As explained earlier, a week before the presidential inaugural, Tenet informed Bush, Cheney, and Rice that bin Laden was a tremendous threat to the United States and that his network was an elusive and difficult target. In March, Clarke warned Rice that domestic or international terrorists might use a truck bomb on Pennsylvania Avenue, and that there might be terrorist cells, including al Qaeda, inside the United States. During the month of April, the CIA picked up intelligence on Abu Zubaydah, a man believed to have been involved in the planning of a number of millennium terror plots. In its reports to Clarke, the CIA indicated that Zubaydah was planning to attack Israel, Saudi Arabia, or India in the "near future." Clarke passed on the information to Rice.[60] In response to these reports, the FBI forwarded a summary of the intelligence to all of its field offices, and asked them to "task all resources for information pertaining to current operational activities relating to Sunni extremism." Its bulletin, however, said nothing about a possible domestic threat.[61]

On April 19, Clarke and members of CSG met to discuss the reports on Zubaydah. They concluded that Zubaydah was planning something, and that he was not alone. That same day, the CSG distributed a briefing to top administration officials entitled "Bin Laden Planning Multiple Operations." The reports in May were equally alarming: "Bin Laden public profile may presage attack" and "Bin Laden network's plans advancing." On May 16, a U.S. embassy received an anonymous phone call warning that bin Laden's supporters intended to launch an attack in the United States using "high explosives." By the end of the month, Clarke was so worried about the nature of the intelligence that he suggested to Rice she ask Tenet what else the United States could do to stop Zubaydah from launching major attacks against Israel and, possibly, U.S. facilities. "When these attacks occur, as they likely will," Clarke stated, "we will wonder what more we could have done to stop them."[62] Clarke restated his concern in a meeting in June attended by security officials of the Federal Aviation Administration (FAA), Immigration, Secret Service, Coast Guard, Customs, and the Federal Protective

Service. Clarke's message was blunt: "You've just heard that CIA thinks al Qaeda is planning a major attack on us. So do I. You heard the CIA say it would probably be in Israel or Saudi Arabia. Maybe. But maybe it will be here. Just because there is no evidence that says that it will be here, does not mean it will be overseas. They may try to hit us at home. You have to assume that is what they are going to do."[63]

Throughout the month of June, the CIA was very busy. On June 12, it circulated a memo entitled "Terrorism: Biographical Information on Bin Laden Associates in Afghanistan." The communiqué stated that a man by the name of Halide Sheikh Mohammed was recruiting people to travel to the United States to meet with colleagues already in the country in order to assist in carrying out plans on bin Laden's behalf. Toward the end of June, the threats grew more colorful. The CIA intercepted communications between bin Laden's operatives declaring things such as "zero hour is tomorrow," or "something spectacular is coming."[64] On June 23, it released a terrorist threat advisory entitled "Possible Threat of Imminent Attack from Sunni Extremists." The CIA explicitly noted that there was a "high probability of near-term 'spectacular' terrorist attacks resulting in numerous casualties."[65]

During the last days of June, the Bush administration received daily CIA briefings with provocative titles such as "Bin Laden Attacks May Be Imminent," "Bin Laden Threats Are Real," and "Bin Laden and Associates Making Near-Term Threats." One of the reports contended that several attacks would most likely ensue in the coming days, among them a "severe blow" to American and Israeli "interests."[66] During the same period, Clarke wrote a memo to Rice in which he noted that an Arabic TV station had stated bin Laden had expressed his pleasure with al Qaeda leaders who were saying the next weeks would "witness important surprises" and that U.S. and Israeli interests would be targeted. Clarke explained that the warnings were too sophisticated to be nothing more than a psychological ruse to keep the United States on edge. On June 28, he drafted another memo, also to the national security adviser, cautioning that the "pattern of al Qaeda activity indicating attack planning over the past six weeks has reached a crescendo . . . A series of new reports continue to convince me and analysts at State, CIA, DIA, and NSA that a major terrorist attack or series of attacks is likely in July." Two days later, the CIA circulated a cable cautioning that something "very, very, very, very" big was about to happen, and that many of bin Laden's followers were eagerly awaiting an attack. It ordered all its station chiefs to share current information with their host governments and to "push for immediate disruption of cells."[67] That same day, top U.S. officials read a document titled "Bin Laden Planning High-Profile Attacks." It stated that bin Laden "operatives expected near-term attacks to have dramatic consequences of catastrophic proportions." In addition, Saudi Arabia moved to its highest terror alert level. In response to the escalated threat reporting, the U.S. Central Command increased the "force protection level" for U.S. troops in the Middle East to the maximum level, moved the U.S. Fifth Fleet out of Bahrain, halted a Marine Corps exercise in Jordan, increased security at all U.S. Embassies in the Persian Gulf, and closed the embassy in Yemen.

Over the next few days, there were indications that increased U.S. security measures had generated problems for al Qaeda. On July 2, the CIA drafted a document named "Planning for Bin Laden Attacks Continues, Despite Delays." It suggested that bin Laden's network had postponed the actual attack, but was continuing the planning. On that same day, the FBI Counterterrorism Division circulated a message to all local, state, and federal law enforcement agencies titled "National Threat Warning System—Potential Anti-U.S. Terrorist Attacks." The memo warned of increased threat reporting from groups "aligned with or sympathetic to Osama bin Laden"; but also noted that the "FBI has no information indicating a credible threat of terrorist attack in the United States." It added, however, that the possibility of such an attack should not be overlooked, and instructed recipients to "exercise extreme vigilance" and "report suspicious activities" to the FBI It did not recommend the taking of any specific action to stop attacks. On July 5, in a briefing to Attorney General Ashcroft on the current situation, a CIA representative stated, "preparations for multiple attacks were in late stages or already complete and that little additional warning could be expected." The update, however, alluded only to threats on U.S. interests abroad. The following day, the CIA warned the CSG that members of bin Laden's network believed the impending attack would be "spectacular, qualitatively different from anything they had done to date." Clarke forwarded the information to Rice and Hadley.[68]

While Washington's top political and bureaucratic figures were trying to decipher, and respond to, the barrage of warning signals coming from a wide range of sources, FBI's field officers were wondering what to infer from a series of developments. On July 10, Kenneth Williams, an agent in the Phoenix field office, described a strange phenomenon. Throughout the summer, Williams had noticed that an "inordinate number of individuals of investigative interest" were enrolled in American civil aviation schools. In a memo he sent to the FBI headquarters in Washington, the agent wrote: "The purpose of this communication is to advise the Bureau and New York of the possibility of a coordinated effort by USAMA BIN LADEN (UBL) to send students to the United States to attend civil aviation universities and colleges . . . The inordinate number of these individuals attending these types of schools . . . gives reason to believe that a coordinated effort is underway to establish a cadre of individuals who will one day be working in the civil aviation community around the world. These individuals will be in a position in the future to conduct terror activity against civil aviation targets."[69]

The memo was not the result of a chance discovery. The previous summer, the Phoenix Field Office had interviewed an individual it considered of "investigative interest" named Zakaria Mustapha Soubra. Zakaria Mustapha was enrolled in a flight school named Embry Riddle University in Prescott, Arizona. The details of the interview were included in the memo:

> SOUBRA stated that he considers the United States Government and U.S. Military forces in the Gulf as "legitimate military targets of Islam." He also stated that the targeting of U.S. Embassies in Africa was "legitimate." SOUBRA denied having received any military training.

However, Phoenix believes that SOUBRA was being less than truthful in this regard. SOUBRA was defiant towards interviewing Agents and it was clear that he was not intimidated by the FBI presence. It is obvious that he is a hardcore Islamic extremist who views the U.S. as an enemy of Islam. Investigation of SOUBRA is continuing . . .

Having outlined the significance of the situation, the Phoenix Field Office issued a series of recommendations to Washington:

Phoenix believes that the FBI should accumulate a listing of civil aviation universities/colleges around the country. FBI field offices with these types of schools in their area should establish appropriate liaison; FBIHQ should discuss this matter with other elements of the U.S. intelligence community and task the community for any information that supports Phoenix's suspicions. FBIHQ should consider seeking the necessary authority to obtain visa information from the USDOS on individuals obtaining visas to attend these types of schools and notify the appropriate FBI field office when these individuals are scheduled to arrive in their area of responsibility.

The FBI did not act on the recommendations of the Phoenix field office prior to September 11. In fact, those responsible for monitoring the activities of al Qaeda and radical fundamentalist groups at the FBI's headquarters in Washington, D.C., did not see the memo until after September 11.

On July 18, as a follow-up on recent and ongoing threat reports, the Department of State issued a public warning of "possible attacks in the Arabian Peninsula." The next day, the acting FBI director Thomas Pickard held a teleconference with all special agents in charge of the various field offices. In his call, he asked that response teams be ready to move at any moment in case of an attack. He did not, however, address the possibility that a plot might be developed inside the United States. On July 25, the CIA presented to top officials a document titled "One Bin Laden Operation Delayed, Others Ongoing." In this document analysts suggested that the CIA had moderately specific intelligence pertaining to a particular plot.[70] The following week, on July 31, the FAA broadcast a communiqué that was disseminated to all federal and private airline programs. The circular informed the aviation community of "reports of possible near-term terrorist operations . . . particularly on the Arabian Peninsula and/or Israel." It went on to state that there was no evidence of a threat to U.S. civil aviation, although some "currently active" terrorist groups were known to "plan and train for hijackings . . ."[71]

High-level officials responded differently to the latest intelligence. Tenet was troubled. The system, he noted, "was blinking red . . . it could not get any worse." Wolfowitz, on the other hand, "questioned the reporting" and suggested to Hadley that "perhaps Bin Laden was trying to study U.S. reactions." Hadley relayed Wolfowitz's skepticism to Tenet, who immediately dismissed it and noted that he "had already addressed the Defense Department's questions on this point." Tenet added that the "reporting was convincing." Two officials in the Counterterrorism Center seemed to concur with Tenet's assessment. More importantly, they were so concerned about the nature of the intelligence, and the disinclination on the part of the Bush administration's top officials to be more attuned to the threats, that they considered resigning in order to disclose their concerns to the public. Ironically, Clarke, who for some time had been one of the most vociferous alarmists, seemed less worried, at least temporarily. In a memo he delivered to Rice and Hadley on July 27 on the current state of the threat, he noted that the "spike in intelligence about a near-term al Qaeda attack has stopped." However, he insisted that the government remain ready throughout the month of August, as a recent report suggested the possibility that plans had been postponed for a few months, "but will still happen."[72]

On August 1, the FBI distributed a memo titled "Third Anniversary of the 1998 U.S. Embassy Bombings in East Africa Approaches; Threats to U.S. Interests Continue." The communiqué echoed previous broadcasts stating that despite having no evidence to claim that an attack inside the United States was about to happen, such a possibility could not be discounted. Two days later, the CIA issued a disconcerting document named "Threat of Impending al Qaeda Attack to Continue Indefinitely." It identified the Arabian Peninsula, Jordan, Israel, and Europe as possible targets, and suggested that al Qaeda was "lying in wait and searching for gaps in security before moving forward with the planned attacks."[73] These memos and documents frequently found their way into the President's Daily Brief (PDB) and became a topic of conversation during the meetings. The president often asked his briefer whether any of the threats pointed to the United States. To prepare a satisfactory answer, a team of CIA analysts was ordered to compile an analysis. Two of the analysts involved in the document's preparation took it as "an opportunity to communicate their view that the threat of a Bin Laden attack in the United States remained both current and serious." On August 6, they had their chance. The lead item in the PDB was titled "Bin Laden Determined to Strike in U.S."[74] This was the 36th PDB item pertaining to bin Laden or al Qaeda in 2001, but it was the first to address the danger of an attack within the United States. Though Bush had known since becoming president that al Qaeda was dangerous and that bin Laden had long been talking and writing about wanting to attack the United States, for him the August 6 PDB item was "historical in nature." And yet, despite the grave concerns articulated in the document, Bush did not order any of his top officials to adopt special measures designed to minimize the probability of an attack inside the United States. He seemed heartened by the knowledge that 70 investigators were attempting to ascertain the exact nature of the threat. His lack of deep concern was best conveyed by the fact that he and his advisers did not address the possibility of an al Qaeda attack inside the United States until the attack had already ensued.[75]

Despite the absence of profound apprehension in the upper echelons of the Bush administration, FBI field officers continued to follow leads. On August 15, the Minneapolis FBI Field Office initiated an investigation of Zacarias Moussaoui, a French national with ties to the Middle East who had begun resuming his flight training at the Pan Am International Flight Academy in Eagan, Minneapolis, two days earlier.[76] From an intelligence standpoint, Moussaoui's activities instantly lit up across the boards. First, agents discovered that he was unqualified to receive flight training on Pan Am's Boeing 747 flight simulators. Most of those who trained on the simulators were current commercial airline pilots, or at least FAA-certified trainees. Moussaoui was neither. When questioned about his lack of qualifications, Moussaoui remarked that he had no intention of becoming a commercial airline pilot. His only reason for the training, he claimed, was that it was an "ego-boosting thing." The investigator's suspicion grew when he learned that Moussaoui, "with little knowledge of flying . . . wanted to learn how to take off and land a Boeing 747"; maintained approximately $32,000 in a bank account but could not explain how, where, or when he had obtained the funds; held jihadist beliefs; and had traveled in recent months to Pakistan, a well-known link for travel to the terrorist training camps in Afghanistan. The agent concluded that Moussaoui was "an Islamic extremist preparing for some future act in furtherance of radical fundamentalist goals," and that his flight training might be a part of his plan.[77]

The same agent then contacted a member of the Minneapolis Joint Terrorism Task Force, who suspected Moussaoui of plotting to hijack an airplane. Together, they forwarded their concerns to the FBI headquarters in Washington. Minneapolis and Washington squabbled back and forth as to whether to detain Moussaoui immediately. The advantage in delaying, argued Washington, was that it allowed Minneapolis to conduct some surveillance on the suspect and perhaps learn more about his plans. Ultimately, Minneapolis decided that the most important thing was that Moussaoui receive no further flight training, which could translate into a possible hijacking. The Immigration and Naturalization Service (INS), after determining that Moussaoui had long overstayed his visa in the United States, detained him. With Moussaoui removed from flight training, the FBI agent in Minneapolis asked permission to search his laptop computer for evidence of a specific plot. Washington rejected the request for a search warrant, claiming that Moussaoui had not committed a crime, other than a visa violation, and that the agent did not have sufficient probable cause.

Frustrated, the Minneapolis agent decided to seek help elsewhere. Under the Foreign Intelligence Surveillance Act (FISA), the FBI can obtain a special search warrant if it can demonstrate that a suspect was an "agent of a foreign power." Because the FBI agent did not have on hand any proof of such a connection, he requested assistance from the FBI's legal attachés in Paris and London on August 18.[78] In the next six days, the agent also contacted a FBI detailee and a CIA desk officer at the Counterterrorist Center regarding the case. The CIA responded by sending a cable on August 24 to London and Paris pertaining to "subjects involved in suspicious 747 flight training." The cable included a segment that described Moussaoui as a possible "suicide hijacker" and asked for any information London or Paris might have. London did not make the FBI's or CIA's requests a priority. However, by August 27, Paris had provided the FBI with information that connected Moussaoui to a Chechen rebel leader named Ibn al Khattab. This information spawned a "spirited debate" between the FBI's Minneapolis field office, its Washington headquarters, and the CIA as to whether Khattab was "sufficiently associated with a terrorist organization to constitute a 'foreign power,' " a qualification necessary to obtain a FISA application. The FBI official in Washington did not think that the connection provided by the French would suffice; therefore, he declined to submit an application. To cover its bases, on September 4, FBI headquarters distributed teletypes to the CIA, the FAA, the Custom Service, the State Department, the INS, and the Secret Service, outlining what it knew about Moussaoui. The report, however, did not include Minneapolis's assessment that Moussaoui intended to hijack a plane. It did contain a comment by the FAA that "it was not unusual for Middle Easterners to attend flight training schools in the United States."[79]

The disparity between the Minneapolis and Washington offices in their assessment of Moussaoui and Washington's was significant. A conversation between a Minneapolis supervisor and a Washington representative illustrates both their divergent perceptions of the situation and the Minneapolis officer's startling foresight. Washington protested that Minneapolis's FISA request was expressed in a manner intended to get people "spun up." The Minneapolis supervisor replied that that was exactly his objective. He was, he explained, "trying to keep someone from taking a plane and crashing into the World Trade Center." Washington replied that nothing like that was going to happen and highlighted that no one knew whether Moussaoui was a terrorist.[80]

At this juncture, the Minneapolis office could have gone up the chain of command at FBI headquarters to discuss the Moussaoui case, but decided against it. The FBI's acting director and assistant director for counterterrorism, thus, were in no position to act on the matter. Paradoxically, though the CIA director was briefed extensively about the Moussaoui case on August 23, he did not consider the possibility that there could be a connection between the suspect and al Qaeda. For this reason, and because he viewed Moussaoui as an FBI case, he never passed the information on to the White House.[81]

A similar form of miscommunication emerged within the FAA, which has its own security branch. Between April and September 10, the FAA received from its security branch some 52 intelligence reports mentioning bin Laden and al Qaeda. Of these five cited al Qaeda's training capability to conduct hijacking and two referred to suicide operations. The FAA continued to assume that if a hijacking were to ensue, it would happen overseas. Nevertheless, in the spring it warned airports that if "the intent of the hijacker is not to exchange hostages for prisoners, but to commit suicide in a spectacular explosion, a domestic hijacking would probably be preferable."[82] None of the warnings, however, included "specific information about means or methods that would have enabled [the FAA] to tailor any countermeasures."[83]

The effects of the various missteps were experienced on September 11. In the early morning, 19 al Qaeda members boarded four U.S. commercial planes, two in Boston, one in Dulles, and one in Newark. All four airplanes were scheduled to fly to the same destination—Los Angeles. The al Qaeda operatives hijacked the aircrafts shortly after departure, and by 10:03 a.m. they had crashed all four—the ones from Boston against the North and South Towers of the World Trade Center in New York, the one from Dulles into the Pentagon in Washington, D.C., and the one from Newark into an empty field in Pennsylvania. Their actions brought about the deaths of nearly 3,000 people.

CHAPTER THREE

THE LOGIC OF SURPRISE VERSUS THE LOGIC OF SURPRISE AVOIDANCE

Saddam Hussein was being very deliberate . . . armored units could not more vividly advertise their intent. It was as if a gun had been loaded and aimed, and a finger put on the trigger.

—Walter P. Lang

It looked like bluster, it looked like an armed threat really for the purpose of achieving some diplomatic or political objective, but it didn't look like an invasion . . .

—Colin Powell

Zero hour is tomorrow.
How could one private person without the resources of a foreign government be such a threat?

—Senator David Boren

Surprise and Surprise Avoidance

A strategy of surprise is the result of calculated decisions made prior to the outbreak of hostilities. It entails the deliberate attempt by one actor to prevent his potential victim from learning beforehand what is being schemed against him.[1] The would-be surpriser can attain surprise in several ways. Whenever possible, he will attempt to disguise both his intention and rationale; that is, he will try to prevent his potential victim from learning what he wants to do and why. Moreover, he may try to conceal his state's true aggregate economic and military strength, and the type, size, location, movement, and readiness of his military forces. Coupled with these dimensions, he may attempt to disguise the military doctrine that will guide the operation. And, whenever possible, a would-be surpriser will make an effort to prevent his potential victim from learning that he is the target and when he will be attacked.[2]

Surprise prevention entails the concurrent execution of disparate tasks. In addition to gaining access to reliable information, the intelligence analyst and the foreign policy-maker of the targeted state need to develop a theory or model of the "adversary's behavioral style and approach to calculating political action."[3] Several obstacles stand in their way of designing an accurate theory or model. First, not every potential aggressor has a well-known history, which can be analyzed thoroughly and systematically. Second, even when such a history is available, an actor may face a potential aggressor with a substantially different belief system. Belief variance hinders the ability of the intelligence analyst and the foreign policy-maker to determine an opponent's approach to utility calculation. More to the point, it encumbers their capacity to determine how an adversary ranks his preferences, to calculate whether his present ranking corresponds with his past one, and to estimate whether his ranking will change in the future.[4] It also undermines their capability to calculate the risks their potential adversary is prepared to take.[5]

Besides these constraints, the intelligence analyst and the foreign policy-maker are regularly hampered by differences in the way each approaches an international problem. The intelligence analyst deals with an international predicament from a relatively narrow vantage point. Based on what he already knows about a potential adversary's behavior and on recently collected information, the intelligence analyst delineates a number of scenarios and assigns to each a subjectively estimated and inexact probability value. The foreign policy-maker, upon receiving the intelligence analyst's assessment, might decide to accept it, question parts of it and ask for a new analysis, or write it off. Though it is impossible to predict what action the foreign policy-maker will take, it is very likely that he will be suspicious of or will outright reject the intelligence analyst's conclusions if they challenge some deeply rooted preconceptions or question an existing policy.

The absence of consensus between intelligence analysts and the failure on the part of an intelligence branch to provide pertinent information to another one can also limit the foreign policy-maker's prospect of preventing a surprise attack. Competing intelligence assessments about a potential aggressor's intentions and actions free the foreign policy-maker of the targeted state to select the analysis that best affirms his preconceptions. However, because in all probability such an assessment was constructed with incomplete information, it jeopardizes the foreign policy-maker's ability to define accurately the problem he is trying to resolve. Lastly, bureaucratic competition frequently compels intelligence organizations to not share critical information with one another. This rivalry sometimes hampers the foreign policy-maker's capacity to comprehend the "true" nature of the challenge his state faces.

An Avertable Surprise

In early 1990, Saddam Hussein concluded that his forces could not invade Kuwait unless he first received an unambiguous assurance from Israel that it would not exploit his decision by initiating an attack of its own against Iraq. The Iraqi leader knew that there was no better way to ascertain the veracity of Israel's pledge than by having Washington act as the conduit of the message. He also understood that he could not afford to infringe on Kuwait's sovereignty without first finding out how Washington might respond. Repeated attempts on his part to decipher the Bush administration's predisposition were followed by assertions by U.S. political leaders and foreign policy-making officials that Washington wanted to strengthen its relationship with Iraq; that it was up to Iraq and Kuwait, with the assistance of other Gulf states, to resolve their differences; and that the United States did not have a security agreement with any of the Arab states. Based on their statements, Saddam Hussein had good reason to conclude that if his forces invaded Kuwait, Washington would not retaliate militarily. This perception was reinforced by his ambassador to the United States who, after monitoring what a number of senior officials in Washington were saying, informed Baghdad that there "were few risks of an American reaction of an intervention in Kuwait."[6]

Saddam Hussein's capacity to masquerade his intentions was limited. He knew that the United States had the means to monitor the deployment of his forces and that, as they got closer to the Kuwaiti border, U.S. intelligence analysts would pass that information on to their superiors, who would then try to decipher his intention. He also recognized that Washington would be troubled by his government's ongoing condemnation of Kuwait's behavior and would wonder how such criticism might be related to the force deployment. Thus, to mislead Washington or, at minimum, to kindle ambiguity about his intention, Saddam Hussein sought the help of his Middle Eastern counterparts, his ambassador to the United States, and the U.S. ambassador to Iraq. Through them, he tried to convey the idea that he was a resolute but practical leader, and that he was deploying his forces not to wage war but to coerce his adversary to acquiesce to his demands. Ultimately, however, Saddam Hussein's strategy was not sufficiently adroit to achieve surprise. It was successful mainly because the first President Bush and his senior advisers refused to reassess their theory of Iraq's behavioral style and approach to calculating risks.

In 1989, Washington welcomed a new administration. Many of its protagonists were not strangers to the city. The new president, George H. W. Bush, had served for eight years as vice president in the previous administration, and before then as CIA director, U.S. representative to China, U.S. ambassador to the United Nations, and congressman. The national security adviser, Brent Scowcroft, had worked in the same capacity under Gerald Ford, and the secretary of state, James A. Baker III, had operated as President Ronald Reagan's chief of staff and subsequently as his secretary of the treasury. Other veteran policy-makers such as Dick Cheney, a Wyoming congressman and chief of staff under President Ford, and General Colin Powell, a deputy national security adviser and national security adviser under President Reagan, were also members of the cast—the former as secretary of defense, the latter as chairman of the Joint Chiefs of Staff.

The new central characters shared a number of beliefs. First, they believed that with the United States just emerging triumphantly from the Cold War, one of its principal tasks would be to foster worldwide order. Second, they felt strongly that it was imperative to infuse the Middle East with a considerable measure of stability. And third, they hoped to persuade the leader of Iraq that it would serve his interests to help stabilize his region. To understand how they derived the third belief and its subsequent effect on their analytical perspective during the days preceding the invasion, it is first necessary to bring to light the Iraqi policy designed by the previous administration.

By 1984, the war between Iraq and Iran was starting to take on a new meaning among a number of senior officials in the Reagan administration. During the early stages, Washington, though critical of Saddam Hussein's ruthless actions against Iraq's Shiite Muslims and ethnic Kurds and his acerbic anti-Israel rhetoric, considered the war an effectual antidote to Iran's Islamic fundamentalists. Washington built the policy on the old adage, "the enemy of my enemy is my friend."[7] Toward the end of 1983, Secretary of State George Shultz and Secretary of Defense Casper Weinberger, concerned that a protracted war or a victory by Iran would badly affect the Middle East and the flow of Persian Gulf oil, urged nations to stop selling weapons to Tehran.

Not everyone in the Reagan administration favored its pro-Iraq/ anti-Iran policy. The president's national security adviser, Robert McFarland, convinced that under the right set of circumstances Washington could turn fundamentalist Iran into a strategic barrier against Soviet influence in the region, presented the idea in a new National Security Decision Directive. With the backing of the CIA director William Casey, McFarland argued that the United States and its allies and friends should "help Iran meet its important requirements so as to reduce the attractiveness of Soviet assistance and tradeoffs, while demonstrating the value of correct relations with the West."[8] McFarland also believed that the sale of weapons to Iran would encourage its leaders to serve as middlemen with groups holding U.S. hostages in Lebanon. Shultz and Weinberger opposed the change in policy. The former contended that permitting or encouraging "a flow of Western arms to Iran is contrary to our interests both in containing Khomeinism and in ending the excesses of the regime. We should not alter this aspect of our policies when groups with ties to Iran are holding U.S. hostages in Lebanon."[9] Weinberger claimed that providing weapons to Iran "would be seen as inexplicably inconsistent by those nations whom we have urged to refrain from such sales," and "would adversely affect our newly emerging relationship with Iraq."[10] The discussion, however, "took place out of sight and mind of Reagan."[11] In August, Reagan authorized McFarland to sell weapons to Iran.

By November of 1986, the world had learned that Reagan had done what he had promised he would never do—bargain with terrorists in order to free hostages. Washington's Middle Eastern friends and allies did not welcome the news. Though they opposed Saddam Hussein's attempt to alter the distribution of power in the Middle East, they feared Iran's drive to export its fundamentalist revolution more. In March 1987, Reagan went on television and acknowledged that his attempt to begin a "strategic opening to Iran had deteriorated, in its implementation, into trading arms for hostages." The policy, he concluded, "was a mistake."[12] Shortly afterward, his administration reverted to its earlier policy of supporting Iraq's war against Iran, while publicly claiming absolute neutrality. Between then and 1988, the United States sold Iraq $240 million worth of military equipment.[13] Ironically, it also played a role in helping Iraq develop its nuclear weapons program.[14]

Washington's new policy remained untouched until the end of the Iraq–Iran war. The incoming administration took its clues from the departing one. The Bush administration decided that it would be in the United States's best interests to try to solidify its relationship with Baghdad. As explained by Scowcroft, in the middle of 1990 we "were not preoccupied with Saddam Hussein. What we hoped was to continue the policy of the Reagan Administration, which was first of all a balance between Iran and Iraq and then hoping perhaps make Saddam Hussein a minimally useful member of the international community. After the Iran/Iraq war, Iraq had enormous reconstruction issues, and it was our hope that American business would be able to participate in that since Iraq fundamentally is a wealthy nation."[15] Baker concurred. The new administration, he noted, "embarked upon a policy of trying to moderate his [Saddam Hussein's] behavior, trying to engage with him, trying to engage politically and economically and in effect bring Iraq into the community of responsible nations."[16]

Frederick the Great claimed that it is pardonable to be defeated in war, but not to be surprised. A reputable intelligence and decision-making analyst challenged his contention, proposing that any party intent on attaining surprise can succeed because the requirements of a successful strategy of deception are not overly demanding.[17] Neither is entirely correct. Because there is no sure method for avoiding surprise, victims of surprise must sometimes be pardoned. And, conversely because the successful implementation of a strategy of deception sometimes can be very demanding, would-be surprisers do not always succeed.

As a world power, the United States monitors and evaluates vast amounts of information coming from different parts of the world. Despite the fact that Washington possesses enormous resources to process great quantities of data, its central foreign policy-makers often lack the time and energy to address carefully and systematically every pending problem. Powell acknowledged as much when he noted that there "are lots of things going on in Washington in any day . . ." He added that the growing evidence of an impending Iraqi invasion "just did not gel early enough for us to deal with [it] as a single problem that required immediate effort on our part . . ."[18]

Powell's apology does not stand up to scrutiny. The first Bush administration was surprised not because it lacked sufficient information, it had little warning, or Saddam Hussein implemented an ingenious strategy of deception. Daily, from July 16 on, the intelligence community provided Bush, Powell, Cheney, Scowcroft, and Haass fresh information and analysis about Saddam Hussein's force deployment. Though initially members of the intelligence community were not of one mind as to the significance of Iraq's troop deployment, some analysts voiced enough concern to warrant a careful reassessment of initial expectations. Specifically, the manner in which Saddam Hussein had positioned his troops should have alerted the Bush administration's senior foreign policy officials that he could use them in a patently more belligerent manner than he claimed he would, and that he might decide to do so.

The Bush administration's reluctance to give credence to the idea that Saddam Hussein might decide to invade Kuwait can be attributed to two interrelated decision-making conditions and to its attitude toward the United States's intelligence-gathering community. First, as already explained, for quite some time its leading foreign policy officials had been trying to convince Saddam Hussein that it would be in their mutual interests to work together to promote stability in the Middle East. Second, acknowledgment that their policy was incongruous with Saddam Hussein's latest confrontational pronouncements and behavior would have required considering the implementation of a new policy laden with domestic and international costs. The Bush administration's top foreign policy officials were averse to reconsidering their Iraqi policy because of the costs that a hostile course of action could have generated. Powell acknowledged this disposition when he noted that the Bush administration's mistake might have been its unwillingness to look a "little harder at those sort of deterrent action." We "were uneasy about starting military actions that might make a bad situation worse."[19]

The decision-making process was also undermined by the propensity on the part of Bush and his closest advisers to place greater weight on the counsel they received from leaders in the Middle East than on the information and analyses educed by the United States's intelligence community. As explained by Scowcroft, though many in the intelligence community had warned him and other senior advisers that they should take seriously Saddam Hussein's force deployment, "we tended to put more stock in [President] Mubarak and [King] Hussein's appraisal than our own."[20] Haass concurred with his boss's explanation. Predictions of "Saddam Hussein's intentions [by U.S. intelligence analysts] didn't impress me a whole hell of a lot and at some point you become your own intelligence analyst for better and for worse. And unlike the intelligence people, people like me on the policy side had a better sense of what the policy dimension of it was so I knew often better than they did what was going in and out of the diplomatic channel and so forth."[21]

In sum, to conclude that Iraq's behavior threatened the interests of the United States the senior members of the Bush administration would have had to reject a policy that had been initiated by the Reagan administration and that they had fully endorsed and pursued and replace it with a more aggressive one.[22] They sought to reinforce their commitment to the original policy with two interrelated justifications. They reasoned that it would be irrational for Saddam Hussein to initiate a new war because of the high price Iraq had paid during its war against Iran. They validated their contention with the claim that well-informed and trusted Middle Eastern leaders were assuring them that the Iraqi leader would not invade Kuwait. During their analysis they failed to consider that Saddam Hussein might have viewed a war against Kuwait as a low-cost endeavor, especially if the United States refrained from becoming involved in it militarily. They also did not bear in mind that Saddam Hussein might have wanted to invade Kuwait in order to reinvigorate his country's economy and regional power. Their stubborn refusal to entertain ideas that might contradict the goals of their original policy was best captured by Haass when he conceded that maybe he and his superiors had become "victims of a mindset. Here it is the post–Cold War world, people are talking about the end of history. Maybe we thought that the era had passed when countries, if you will . . . with all their military force and simply tried to erase other countries off the map. Maybe it was simply too big of a thought for us to comfortably absorb."[23]

A More Challenging Surprise-Avoidance Task

Throughout the summer of 2001, the intelligence community in the United States was repeatedly frustrated by its access to a wealth of incomplete information. When reports did not specify a target, intelligence officials assumed the threat was overseas; when the accounts did not specify the method the hijackers might use to commandeer the plane, the officials did not consider the possibility that they might use highly rudimentary instruments.[24] Their two most significant oversights were the mishandling of the "Phoenix Memo" and the refusal on the part of the FBI official in Washington to pursue the investigation of Zacarias Moussaoui more aggressively.

The Phoenix Memo was not specific in nature. Its author noted that the memo "was not an alert about suicide pilot . . . [it] was more about a Pan Am Flight 103 scenario in which explosives were placed on an aircraft." Viewed in isolation, thus, none of the information provided in the memo would have been enough to foil the plot. The writer of the memo, however, requested that his information be distributed among other field officers. If indeed the memo had been read, and its recommendations followed, it might well have placed the investigation of Moussaoui in August in a vastly different light. This compels us to ask: could a different mindset at the White House have enhanced the probability that someone in the intelligence community would have established a link between the two sources?

In Washington, where every incoming administration is immediately exposed to a barrage of international challenges, the likelihood that it will be attentive right away to a particular set of warnings is largely a function of whether in its initial foreign policy agenda it identified the instigator of the signals as a viable threat. It would be disingenuous, however, to contend that, based on the information it had, the second Bush administration should have averted the September 11, 2001 attacks. Al Qaeda's operatives sought to achieve surprise along dimensions favored by insurgent groups: location, means, and time. Without precise information, the potential target faces great difficulty conjecturing any of them, much less all three. And yet, despite al Qaeda's advantages, the Bush administration had enough information to improve noticeably its capability to prevent the September 11 attacks.

As explained earlier, every surprise attack begins with an intention and a rationale. Al Qaeda's leader never sought to disguise either. The

United States's leading counterterrorist figures understood the significance of both and conveyed their concerns frequently to the incoming administration. However, because the new administration came to office convinced that its central task in the post–Cold War era would be to solidify and augment the power of the United States, it had difficulty grasping that non-state insurgents determined to explode a bomb in the middle of a major American city also posed a major threat. Though Bush and his senior foreign policy advisers believed that a new counterterrorism policy had to be designed and organized, they were not deeply alarmed by Osama bin Laden and al Qaeda's actions, and thus a new policy was not their priority. As conceded by the president, "I was not on point . . . I knew he [Osama bin Laden] was a menace, and I knew he was a problem. I knew he was responsible, or felt he was responsible, for the [previous] bombings that killed Americans . . . But I didn't feel that sense of urgency . . ." Or, as a former Clinton official put it, "terrorism wasn't on their plate of key issues."[25]

Had the second Bush administration been markedly more inclined to think of Osama bin Laden and al Qaeda as noteworthy menaces, the government would have allocated greater resources to the task of averting a direct terrorist attack in the United States, agents in the field would have searched for clues more diligently, supervisors at headquarters would have been more attentive to the needs of field agents, the CIA and the FBI would have been more willing to share pertinent information not only internally but also with each other, and their leaders would have been more disposed to share their concerns with the principal decision-makers. In short, despite the fact that the implementation of these measures could have not guaranteed the foiling of the attackers' plans, it would have reduced vastly their likelihood of success.

A First Wrap Up

The earlier analysis compels one to ask: why, when presented with information that indicated that there might be problems with their respective policies, did both administrations refuse to review them thoroughly and systematically? It would seem reasonable to assume that when faced with information that casts doubt on the efficacy of a policy, the rational foreign policy-maker will want to reevaluate it. This reevaluation could force him to conclude that he must consider replacing the policy. The costs and benefits, along with the levels of risks he assigns to alternative policies, will determine whether he decides to do so. In other words, he will choose to change his policy only if he can find another that in his estimation will have a greater expected utility, at an acceptable level of risk.[26]

In the next to last section of chapter one we noted that decision-making theorists have approached this issue from opposing perspectives. One group has proposed that when a foreign policy-maker is pressed to evaluate an existing policy, he never looks beyond a small subset of alternatives, and within each alternative he evaluates only a small number of dimensions. Moreover, when comparing a small range of alternatives, the foreign policy-maker first measures by how much the positive dimension of each alternative compensates its negative dimension and then chooses the alternative with the highest compensatory value. Thus, a foreign policy-maker, faced with the possibility of having to renounce an existing policy, will compare its compensatory value with that of a small set of alternatives and replace it only if the compensatory value of one of the alternatives outmatches it.[27]

A second group of theorists focuses on the cognitive impediments to rationality. From this group has emerged a school of thought that contends that the decision about whether to replace an existing policy is based not on a compensatory calculus but on a non-compensatory process. The foreign policy-maker does not rely on rules "that require the evaluation and comparison of all alternatives across different dimensions . . ." Instead, he relies on a perspective that enables him to adopt or reject "alternatives on the basis of one or a few criteria."[28] In other words, when two important dimensions are present in an alternative and one is negative, the foreign policy-maker, instead of comparing the extent to which the positive dimension compensates the negative one in each alternative, typically rejects any alternative that has a negative dimension.

A comparison of the measures undertaken by the two Bush administrations to uncover what two international entities intended to do and how they planned to attain their objectives reveal a critical similarity, which is best illustrated by the noncompensatory model. Specifically, it captures their nonholistic approach to foreign policy-making. In both instances, rather than conducting a comprehensive and intricate comparison of its preferred policy with another one, the leading decision-makers of each administration stuck with their original design by highlighting, simultaneously, its positive element and the negative component of a possible alternative. They refused to confer sufficient credence to the warnings that an international actor might be prepared to initiate a major act of aggression—one that could severely afflict the interests of the United States—chiefly because such an acknowledgment would have forced them to reformulate their original foreign policy frameworks.

In the case of the first Bush administration, when its senior foreign policy officials were presented with information that could have obliged them to reassess their Iraqi policy, they chose not to initiate a systematic and thorough review. Neither Bush nor any of his senior advisers tried to derive compensatory values for different alternatives, compare them, and choose the one with the largest measure. Instead, when they considered, albeit quite briefly, whether they should supplant the existing Iraqi policy with a forceful and unambiguous deterrence strategy, they dismissed the idea based on the belief (as opposed to a systematically derived estimate) that its implementation could engender high domestic and international political costs. In the words of a senior foreign policy official in the Bush administration, "We were reluctant to draw a line in the sand. I [could not] see the American public supporting the deployment of troops over a dispute over 20 miles of territory and it is not clear that local countries would have supported that kind of commitment."[29]

The second Bush administration responded as poorly to emerging challenges to its security strategy. When presented with information that could have required it to be markedly more attentive to possible al Qaeda threats, its principal members had two additional reasonable options. They could have: (i) adopted immediately and in full the approach to counterterrorism designed by the Clinton administration, or (ii) continued to implement the counterterrorism policy created by the Clinton administration while it devised its own. There is no guarantee that the execution of either one would have been enough to prevent the September 11 attacks. Nevertheless, had the leading members of the second Bush administration chosen either, they would have had a policy—something to guide their actions and those of specialists responsible for tracking al Qaeda operatives and their activities. And yet, the Bush administration's central actors automatically dismissed the implementation of either alternative and decided, instead, to develop a new counterterrorist policy from scratch. They rejected the other two options not because they compared poorly with the third one (there was nothing to compare them with), but because each one carried an unacceptably high negative dimension—the endorsement, even temporarily, of a policy created by the Clinton administration. Doing the opposite of whatever the previous administration had done became early on the second Bush administration's prevalent theme.[30] In the words of Richard Clarke, the "new administration thought Clinton's recommendation that eliminating al Qaeda be one of their highest priorities, well, rather odd, like so many of the Clinton administration's actions, from their perspective."[31] Thus, rather than assessing how the adoption of either option would have compared against developing an entirely new strategy, the second Bush administration impulsively concluded that the temporary lack of a policy was preferable to the implementation of one that had been developed by its predecessor.

Despite the considerable explanatory merit of the noncompensatory model, it has a major shortcoming. The model, as explained earlier, is built on the assumption that there are cognitive limitations to rationality. Though such a contention is valid, the aggregation of the limitations prevents the analysts from being able to identify which ones are actually at play in any one particular decision. In the case of the first Bush administration, one of its gravest errors was to assume that Saddam Hussein would recognize how costly the invasion of

Kuwait would prove both to him and to his country. Its core figures took it for granted that the Iraqi leader would conclude, just as they had, that after having paid a very high cost during the war against Iran, it would be unwise to engage in another war. As they derived such an inference, they failed to consider the possibility that Saddam Hussein might have been using different values to gauge the costs, benefits, and risks that the assault on Kuwait would engender.

Foreign policy-makers, like most humans, too often refuse to acknowledge new realities, even when the information tells them that they should. Sometimes it is only after a costly crisis that they are able to accept that the world in which they interact is no longer the world they had envisioned. The central leaders of the second Bush administration, most of who had played significant roles during the final days of the Cold War, had great difficulty adjusting to the idea that non-state actors, such as terrorist groups, could play a decisive role in the world system. The attacks altered their mindset.

CHAPTER FOUR
TWO VERY DIFFERENT WARS

Introduction

"War is the province of chance. In no other sphere of human activity must such a margin be left for this intruder. It increases the uncertainty of every circumstance and deranges the course of events."[1] Karl von Clausewitz's warning is still fitting. War must never be initiated before its makers examine thoroughly its possible consequences. Too often, however, international leaders have instinctively favored Clausewitz's better-know maxim, "War is a continuation of policy by other means" over the previous aphorism. The intent of this chapter is to describe the manner in which the two Bush administrations addressed this challenge—the first one when it learned that Saddam Hussein's forces had marched into Kuwait, the second when it decided to overthrow the Iraqi leader's regime and replace it with a democratic one.

The Gulf War

The First Phase

The official story that came out of Iraq on August 2, 1990 was a fabrication. Baghdad claimed that a coup had taken place in Kuwait and that its deposed leader had called on Iraq for assistance. The Bush administration was not fooled, but the action still compelled it to formulate a definition of the challenge it faced. Its most immediate task was to assess the effects, if any, that an unanswered Iraqi annexation of Kuwait would have on U.S. domestic and international interests.

Washington also needed to gauge the probability that Saddam Hussein's forces would march into Saudi Arabia and the overall repercussion of such an action. If it were to calculate that the impact of the first incident, or both, would be substantial, it would have to design and articulate a response.

The U.S. government always has a wide range of contingency plans, which it can activate at a moment's notice. It did not have a planned response to an Iraqi invasion of Kuwait in 1990. Central Command (CENTCOM), the U.S. organization responsible for military action in the Gulf region, had been designing one, but it remained unfinished. What is more, CENTCOM did not have, in or near the region, the military apparatus and personnel necessary to mount an effective campaign against Saddam Hussein's forces.[2] The Bush administration's senior foreign policy officials were aware of the impediments limiting the U.S. ability to react promptly when they gathered at the White House 12 hours after the start of the Iraqi invasion.

During the first meeting, President Bush said little and allowed his advisers to explore the problem on their own. They focused principally on whether Saddam Hussein intended to withhold Iraqi and Kuwaiti oil or try to flood the world market. They were greatly concerned with the extent to which the Iraqi leader's influence on the oil market would be augmented if he were to march his troops into Saudi Arabia. Domination of 40 percent of the world's oil reserves by Iraq was a scenario that no one in the room found acceptable. They also evaluated the idea of imposing economic sanctions on Iraq. By the end of the meeting they had accomplished little. This indecision generated different concerns among a few of the attendees. Powell was alarmed by their inability to come up with a clear definition of the problem. Haass was troubled by the failure to discuss in any detail the idea of sending troops halfway around the world.[3] Following the meeting, Haass approached Scowcroft to express his dissatisfaction. The national security adviser calmed him down and said: "There's going to be another meeting, get us ready for that; I am with you. Don't worry about me, don't worry about the President, but do what you have to do."[4]

Shortly after the White House gathering, Bush left for Aspen, Colorado, for a previously scheduled get-together with Britain's prime minister Margaret Thatcher. During the flight, Scowcroft expressed his apprehension about the earlier meeting to the president and requested that at the next gathering he be permitted to speak first in order to outline "the absolute intolerability of this invasion to U.S. interests."[5] Bush agreed, but countered with the suggestion that he make the statement. Scowcroft disagreed on the grounds that it "might stifle discussion." The president accepted Scowcroft's advice. In the meantime, Haass carried out his boss's order. He wrote a memo in which he noted, "The necessary instruments of such a policy [to expel Iraq from Kuwait] would be exports, other economic sanctions, and enhanced military actions, both unilateral and with others."[6]

In Aspen, Thatcher wasted little time in telling Bush that Saddam's incursion had to be stopped and that the only way to persuade the Iraqi leader that his action was unacceptable was by sending troops to the region. Bush concurred.[7] The two leaders also agreed that the future of Kuwait was not the only thing at stake.[8] By then they knew that they could count on some type of support from the United Nations—earlier that day, its Security Council had approved Resolution 660 unanimously. The declaration called on Kuwait and Iraq to address their differences via intense negotiations, and invoked Articles 39 and 40 of chapter seven of the United Nations's Charter. Chapter seven conferred on the United Nations's leading powers the use of economic sanctions or military force to prevent acts of aggression.[9] At that stage, however, the president remained guarded about his plans. During the press conferences after his talk with Thatcher, Bush stated, "We're not ruling any options in, but we're not ruling any options out."[10]

The tone of the discussion between Bush and his senior advisers was measurably different at the August 3 NSC meeting. As he and the president had agreed, Scowcroft delivered the opening remarks. "I detected a note at the end [of the previous NSC meeting] that we might have to acquiesce in an accommodation [with Iraq]," said the national security adviser. "My personal judgment is that the stakes in this for the United States are such that to accommodate Iraq should not be a policy option."[11] Conscious that Scowcroft would not have made the statement unless he had discussed it earlier with the president, and that the national security adviser had signaled in no uncertain terms that the United States had to be prepared to use its military might to offset Saddam Hussein's action, Cheney decided it was imperative to clarify the problems the United States faced. "Initially," said the secretary of defense, "we should sort this out from our strategic interests in Saudi Arabia and oil. Saddam has clearly done what he had to do to dominate OPEC, the Gulf, and the Arab world. He is 40 kilometers from Saudi Arabia and its oil production is only a couple 100 kilometers away. If he doesn't take it physically, with his new wealth he will have an impact and will be able to acquire new weapons. The problem will get worse, not better. Looking at the military possibilities and options, we should not underestimate the U.S. military forces we would need to be prepared for a major conflict."[12] Lawrence Eagleburger, the deputy secretary of state standing in for Secretary of State Baker who was in the Soviet Union, argued that allowing Saddam Hussein to get away with the invasion would set "all the wrong standards" for the post–Cold War period. Inaction, concluded Eagleburger, would inform other dictators that they could get away with aggression.[13] The sole mildly dissenting voice in the meeting came from Powell. Worried about the direction of the discussion, he remarked somewhat sarcastically, "Good, you know, we are going to draw a line in the sand now. Does everybody agree it's worth going to war to reverse the invasion of Kuwait."[14] Powell's observation did not sit well with the other members, and the chairman of the Joint Chiefs of Staff realized, and accepted, that he was not there to involve himself in political discussions but to present military scenarios.

By the time the discussion had come to an end, its participants had a clearer vision of what Bush was prepared to do. They recognized that though the president had said little, he was the one driving the agenda. As explained by Scowcroft, they also understood Bush had made up his mind that "force would be used if necessary, and that planning should be based on the assumption that sanctions would fail."[15] Eagleburger expanded with the contention that by taking a strong stand at the outset, the president had set the parameters within which the discussions would be carried out and, as a result, limited the number of options the participants could consider.[16]

On the afternoon of August 3, Bush moved assertively on a different front. Conscious that a belligerent policy against Iraq depended heavily on Saudi Arabia's readiness to accept U.S. troops on its own territory, he invited the Saudi ambassador to the United States to the White House. Bush's main challenge was to convince Amir Bandar bin Sultan that if Riyadh invited the United States to deploy its forces on Saudi territory, Washington would not retreat at the first sign that things were not going well. The Saudi leadership still remembered the Reagan administration's retreat following the attack on the U.S. Marines stationed in Beirut in 1983. Saudi Arabia's leaders, moreover, worried that the deployment of U.S. forces on the land that housed Islam's holiest sites would incite intense criticism from Muslim fundamentalists.[17] Mindful of what he was asking the Saudis to do, the president said to Bandar, "I give my word of honor . . . I will see this through with you."[18] To ensure that the Saudi ambassador took his message seriously, the president sent him to see Cheney and Powell.

Prior to the second meeting, Scowcroft phoned Cheney to inform him that Bush had ordered Bandar be shown the plan the Pentagon was designing to protect Saudi Arabia, as well as the top-secret satellite photos showing Iraqi forces pointing toward Saudi Arabia. Cheney, an old hand at political and bureaucratic battles, was one of the first to grasp the depth of Bush's commitment to using force if required. However, the secretary of defense concluded that before he and Powell met with Bandar he would have to make it clear to his chief military adviser that it was time to show the Pentagon's plans, regardless of how unclear the military objectives might still seem.

Powell, also a political and bureaucratic veteran, understood that despite his concerns he was expected to follow orders. As he saw it, in a democracy, "it is the President, not generals, who make[s] decisions about going to war . . ."[19] At the meeting, Bandar was informed about Operation Plan 90-1002 and the 100,000–200,000 troops the United States was prepared to deploy if the Saudi leadership authorized Washington to do so.[20] That same afternoon, during a press conference, the president decided not to mince words. "I view very seriously our determination to reverse out this aggression . . . This will not stand. This will not stand, this aggression against Kuwait."[21]

The next morning, Bush and his senior political and military advisers gathered at Camp David to listen to the generals. Powell opened the meeting with an explanation of the rationale behind Operation 90-1002. He noted that it was both a "deterrence piece and a war-fighting piece." General Schwarzkopf then discussed the specifics of the operation. He remarked that it would take 17 weeks to put into operation the deterrence aspect of the plan and that it would involve the deployment of some 200,000–250,000 Army, Air Force, Navy, and Marine personnel. He added that complete preparation for the offensive side of the operation would take 8–12 months.[22] Next they considered whether Washington should focus on liberating Kuwait or protecting Saudi Arabia. Uncomfortable with the idea of engaging U.S. forces in an offensive war, Powell noted that if Iraq were to be expelled from Kuwait, the United States might be forced to change the political and social conditions of the newly freed country. Bush's immediate reply was, "That's why our defense of Saudi Arabia has to be the focus."[23]

At the end of the Camp David gathering, one question still remained unanswered: would Saudi Arabia agree to the deployment of U.S. forces on its territory? On August 5, the Saudi king, after initially rejecting the idea of a U.S. presence on his land, told Bush that he wanted a U.S. team to brief him. Bush immediately dispatched Cheney and an entourage composed of Schwarzkopf; Scowcroft's second in command Robert Gates; Wolfowitz; Cheney's press secretary Peter Williams; the U.S. ambassador to Saudi Arabia

Charles W. Freedman; and two lower ranking officials. Bush's marching order to the group was clear-cut: to convince the Saudi king to authorize the deployment of U.S. forces on his territory. On August 6, after being briefed by Cheney and Schwarzkopf about the Pentagon's military plan and told that some 70,000 Iraqi troops were near, or moving toward, the Saudi border, King Fahd assented. The secretary of defense immediately conveyed the news to Bush, who then told him to stop in Egypt and Morocco to inform its leaders about the latest developments and that soon they would be asked to participate in the defense of Saudi Arabia.[24] The president also authorized Cheney to start the deployment of U.S. forces.

By the time the Saudi king had granted his consent, the United Nations had passed Resolution 661, which authorized the imposition of a trade and financial embargo on Iraq.[25] In the meantime, another very important meeting was about to take place in Baghdad. Troubled by reports from Washington that his forces were moving toward the Saudi border, Saddam Hussein ordered the release of an official statement: "Some news agencies have reported fabricated news about what they called the approach of Iraqi forces towards the Saudi border. Iraq categorically denies these fabricated reports. Causing confusion between the kingdom of Saudi Arabia, which is a fraternal country with which we have normal cordial relations, and Kuwait's case is tendentious."[26] The Iraqi leader then requested a visit from Joseph Wilson, the U.S. Chargé d'Affaires in Baghdad. After lecturing Wilson about Kuwait's economic war against Iraq, Saddam Hussein adopted a more conciliatory tone. He stated: "Iraq is firmly willing to respect the United States's legitimate international interests in the Middle East, and is interested in establishing normal relations with the United States on the basis of mutual respect." He also explained that Iraq and Saudi Arabia had had excellent relations since 1975 and that there was no reason for Riyadh to fear an Iraqi attack.[27]

Bush did not take Saddam Hussein's conversation with Wilson seriously. On August 7, the president ordered a massive U.S troop buildup. The only Congressional leader the president informed beforehand of his intention was Senator Sam Nunn (D-GA), chairman of the Armed Services Committee.[28] The following day Bush delivered an unambiguous message on national television: all Iraqi forces must withdraw from Kuwait.[29] President Bush's speech marked the end of the first phase of the decision-making process that ensued among the highest members of his administration following Iraq's invasion of Kuwait.

The Second Phase

On October 30, the president met with the secretaries of state and defense, the national security adviser, and the chairman of the Joint Chiefs of Staff. Scowcroft began the meeting by noting that the United States was "at a 'Y' in the road" and that it could continue to deter and defend, or it could begin to develop the capability necessary to attack. Powell, who was the next speaker, stated that if the president wanted to go the offensive route, the troops in the Middle East would have to be doubled. The chairman added that Schwarzkopf had called for such an increase and that he supported the request. Cheney concurred and went further. It was not a question of whether to go the offensive route—the president should want that option and order its implementation immediately. Bush's response was to the point: "If that's what you need, we'll do it."[30] The president gave his formal approval the following day.

It is difficult to identify the exact time Bush decided that the United States would have to use force against Iraq to expel its forces from Kuwait, but it is possible to demonstrate that the president made up his mind long before the end of October. A good starting point is the views of his core advisers. According to Powell, who had doubts about going to war in order to force Iraq out of Kuwait, the president was the "spark plug and fuel" of the post-August 2 U.S. foreign policy toward Iraq. Bush's closest foreign policy adviser, Scowcroft, conceded that the president had "made up his mind fairly early on that force would be used if necessary and that planning should be based on the assumption that sanctions would fail." Baker, one of Bush's oldest colleagues, concurred with Scowcroft. The president's "role was absolutely critical. He made a visceral decision to reverse the invasion and he was out in front of all his advisers."[31]

Signs that Bush was prepared to use military force against Iraq, if necessary, began to emerge shortly after the invasion of Kuwait. On August 3, at the NSC meeting, the president openly supported Scowcroft's assertion that the United States could not and would not accept "the invasion of Kuwait" as "an accomplished fact." Bush reiterated the view the following day during his meeting with the Kuwaiti emir Sheikh Jabir al Ahmed al Sabah. The United States, promised the president, would help free Kuwait and place the emir back in power.[32] As if to ensure that no one would question his resolve, Bush proclaimed in public on August 5 that he was determined "to reverse this [Iraqi] aggression . . ."[33] For Powell, the president's public statement was a defining moment. "[F]or me anyway," explained Powell, the statement was "the first expression from the President that he has crossed the line and there's no question he will do what is necessary to get the Iraqis out of Kuwait . . . For me it was a new mission."[34]

Just as Bush was elevating his rhetoric, the Air Force was proposing a new radical air campaign. Under the leadership of Colonel John Warden, an iconoclastic Air Force officer, a top-secret group working inside the Pentagon had been developing a "parallel bombing" campaign. During World War II, the allied forces had relied on "serial bombing" to destroy targets in Germany. In order to inflict heavy damage on a target, a large number of bombers would hit it for a week and then move on to a different one. This approach usually enabled the Germans to repair the earlier target while the allied forces were hitting the second one. The technology of the early 1990s allowed the United States to hit with tremendous precision 50 or 60 targets in just a few hours. It provided the United States the opportunity to destroy Iraq's air power, air defense system, and communication system in less than a week. Warden briefed Schwarzkopf about his plan, who in turn presented it to Cheney and Powell in late August.[35]

As preparations continued to gather momentum, some of Bush's closest advisers began to worry about his growing impatience. On September 16, in a speech to the Iraqi people, the president made it clear that the world would end its sanctions on Iraq when "Iraq returns to the path of peace, when Iraqi troops withdraw from Kuwait, when the country's rightful government is restored, [and] when all foreigners held against their will are released . . ." On October 9, he reiterated his original argument by noting that though his administration would give sanctions a chance to have their intended effect, it "will not let this aggression stand. Iraq will not be permitted to annex Kuwait. And that's not a threat, it's not a boast, it's just the way it's going to be."[36] It was during this time that Schwarzkopf expressed the belief that the United States should not set up a deadline for sanctions to work. "Now we are starting to see evidence that sanctions are pinching. So why should we say, 'Okay, gave 'em two months, didn't work. Let's get on with it and kill a whole bunch of people?' That's crazy. That's crazy . . ."[37]

Powell was more discreet than Schwarzkopf in voicing his concern. He first approached Cheney to see whether he could convince the secretary of defense to ask the president to give sanctions and containment a chance. The general, however, did not succeed. "I don't know," said Cheney, "I don't think the President will buy it." Containment, explained Cheney, would signify that Iraq would retain control over Kuwait, and Bush could not accept that outcome. Moreover, the president could not tolerate the new status quo because he had deemed it unacceptable publicly. Next, Powell approached Scowcroft and presented the case for containment, but without stating that he favored this alternative. The national security adviser was frank in his response. "The President is more and more convinced that sanctions are not going to work." He added that he did not think that Bush would change his mind. Powell still did not give up. In early October, Cheney, though he had already admonished the general for not limiting his input to military issues, took him to see the president for a private talk. During the meeting, Powell noted that there were two ways the United States could force

Saddam out of Kuwait: (i) prepare for an offense by increasing the troops in the region; or (ii) carry on with the policy of containment and the imposition of sanctions. The second one, continued Powell, "is an option that has merit. It will work some day. It may take a year, it may take two years, but it will work some day." He concluded by saying: "Where do you want me to go, Mr. President? As each day goes by, I am doing more. There are more and more troops going in." Bush did not have to think long before he stated where he wanted to go. "I don't think there is time politically for that strategy."[38] Bush's willingness to take a firm stand without an open discussion of alternatives surprised Wolfowitz. As the undersecretary of defense for policy, Wolfowitz was struck by the absence of a process of writing alternatives and implications so that the principal foreign policy-makers could evaluate them.[39]

Top Pentagon officials were not the only ones concerned with Bush's approach to the problem. Baker, who had worked assiduously to persuade the United Nations to authorize an international blockade on Iraq and had ordered the Department of State to develop a document explaining the advantages of containment and sanctions, feared that the Bush administration was speeding toward an armed conflict with Iraq without first garnering public support. The American public, he believed, was not terribly concerned about the plight of Kuwait or Iraq's control over vast amounts of oil.[40] Moreover, Iraq was vulnerable to sanctions and time was "on the side of the international community."[41]

During this period, Baghdad did little to allay Bush's misgivings. On September 21, the Iraqi Revolutionary Command Council challenged the deployment of forces by the coalition, and warned that Iraq would not retreat and was prepared to engage in the "mother of all battles." The next day, Baghdad upped the ante by announcing that if the embargo began to strangle Iraq, it would attack Saudi Arabia and Israel. On October 5, Iraq's foreign minister went before the UN General Assembly and made it clear that his country had no intention of compromising.[42] At around this time, the emir of Kuwait met with Bush and described to him in "quiet, almost understated terms" the way Iraq was dismantling and depopulating Kuwait through murder, rape, torture, and emigration. News about Iraq's horrific behavior so infuriated Bush that it reinforced his predisposition to view the problem in a personal way.[43] Prior to the emir's departure, Bush told him that he would keep all "options open to ensure Iraq's unlawful occupation of Kuwait is ended, and Kuwait's legitimate government secured." Scowcroft sought to reassert the president's sentiment when he spoke to reporters after the meeting. Iraq's system of destruction, warned the national security adviser, was accelerating the possibility of war. "[W]hat is happening inside Kuwait affects the timetable."[44]

As October moved along, planners at the Pentagon prepared for a war that seemed inevitable. On October 10, CENTCOM officials presented war draft plans to top U.S. military leaders in the Pentagon. They repeated their performance at the White House the next day. Following the presentation, Bush asked what the armed forces would need for a full offense. When told, he said that he would soon decide whether to transform the defensive operation into an offensive one.[45] As already noted, he made the formal decision to deploy additional forces on October 30. A meeting held the day before by members of the UN Security Council strengthened the president's resolve. Troubled by the failure on the part of several missions to persuade Saddam Hussein to exit Kuwait peacefully, the Security Council discussed additional alternatives but did not forward a helpful recommendation.[46] That same day, Baker noted during a speech that the Bush administration "would not rule out a possible use of force if Iraq continues to occupy Kuwait."[47]

Members of the media and Congress, in the meantime, began to voice concerns about the steps the Bush administration was taking. Conservatives such as Jeanne Kirkpatrick, Robert Novak, Patrick Buchanan, and George Will wondered about the logic of deploying U.S. forces on Saudi territory.[48] Their voices resonated in Congress. According to the War Powers Resolution passed in 1973, the President must consult with Congress "in every possible instance" before deploying forces into hostilities (section 3). The resolution also stipulated that the president must hand in a written report to Congress no later than 48 hours after U.S. forces have been deployed into hostilities, and withdraw the troops within 60 days after submitting the report. The forces can stay for an additional 30 days if the president informs Congress that the presence of the troops is still necessary.[49] Democrats and several leading Republican leaders, such as Senate Minority Leader Robert Dole and Senator Richard Lugar, demanded that Congress be consulted if the administration intended to place U.S. forces in harm's way, and reminded the president that he did not have the freedom to go to war without its formal authorization. The White House's response was that the president, as the commander in chief, has sufficient power to initiate hostilities without a formal authorization from Congress.[50]

In early November, a couple of days after the midterm congressional elections, Bush announced that he had ordered the secretary of defense to double the number of U.S. forces in the Gulf "to ensure that the coalition has an adequate offensive military option, should that be necessary to achieve our common goal."[51] Initial estimates, he added, suggested that by early 1991 the United States would have some 390,000 troops in the region. Many members of Congress were appalled that the president had acted without consulting its leadership.[52] Among them there were those who were troubled by the fact that though they had met with the president just before he made the decision to double the U.S. forces, and had warned him to "be cautious before [leading] the country to war," he had not disclosed his intention.[53] On November 10, Senate Majority Leader George Mitchell (D-ME) cautioned the president to ask Congress "for a declaration." "If he does not get it," added Mitchell, "then there is no legal authority for the United States to go to war."[54] In an attempt to appease Congress, Bush met with its leaders on November 14. Confronted with the contention that the additional deployment made war inevitable, the president was willing only to promise that he would consult with Congress were he to decide that the use of force was necessary. Less than a week later, dissatisfied with the president's assurance, five congressmen tried to get an injunction that would restrict his freedom to start a war without congressional approval.[55]

In the meantime, the Bush administration continued to move unfalteringly along the road to war. In early October, Baker had asked the Deputies Committee to outline a UN resolution. After extensive discussions, the members of the committee and Baker concluded that the draft should not include a demand for immediate action or the word "ultimatum." They agreed, however, that it should contain the phrase "all necessary means, including military force." Following the president's decision to double the U.S. forces in the Persian Gulf, and with Britain on board, Baker began a series of trips designed to garner support for the U.S. resolution from other critical international actors. During a meeting in Cairo on November 6, the secretary of state convinced the Chinese foreign minister to abstain when the resolution came to a vote. A few days later, he persuaded Russia's president and its foreign minister to back the measure. Determined to have a sufficient majority, Baker also met with the non-permanent members of the UN Security Council. He was not entirely successful—Cuba's and Yemen's representatives made it clear that they would not support the resolution.[56] During this period, the president traveled to the Middle East to also help lay the foundation for a UN resolution. On November 23, after meeting the leaders of Saudi Arabia, Egypt, and Syria, Bush announced that a final agreement on a UN resolution was "very near."[57]

Six days later, by a vote of 12 to 2, the UN Security Council passed Resolution 678. The decree noted that Iraq was given until January 15, 1991 to comply fully with the resolutions already passed regarding the conflict between Kuwait and itself. It also emphasized that if Iraq failed to meet the stipulated terms by the specified date, states cooperating with the government of Kuwait had the authority to "use all necessary means to uphold and implement" the resolutions and "restore international peace and security in the area."[58]

By this time, public opinion in the United States was divided. Notable public figures such as former secretary of state Henry Kissinger and former UN ambassador Jeanne Kirkpatrick argued that Iraq's invasion of Kuwait justified the use of force against the invader. Kissinger remarked that though the "military option would prove painful and difficult," such dangers had to be "weighed against the risk of an even larger conflict later on if a demonstration of American impotence leads to a collapse of moderate governments, to escalating crises and the disintegration of all order." Opposition to the use of force came from several sources. Admiral William Crowe, former chairman of the Joint Chiefs of Staff, testified that though he firmly believed Saddam Hussein had to leave Kuwait, the United States "should give sanctions a fair chance before [it discards] them . . ." Former national security adviser Zbigniew Brzezinski contended that Iraq "has been deterred, ostracized and punished." He added, "[N]either an American war to liberate Kuwait nor a preventive war to destroy Iraq's power is urgently required, be it in terms of the American national interest or of the imperatives of world order . . ." Former secretary of defense James Schlesinger warned that the "sight of the United States inflicting a devastating defeat on an Arab country from the soil of an Arab neighbor may result in an enmity directed at the United States for an extended period."[59]

Aware that his decision to double the U.S. forces in the Persian Gulf and the passage of UN Resolution 678 had created substantial concern among a wide range of military and foreign policy experts outside his administration, and eager to persuade most Americans that no stone was being left unturned, Bush authorized Baker to meet with Iraq's foreign minister in Baghdad. The president, moreover, wanted to make sure that Iraq's foreign minister would understand that the United States was serious about restoring Kuwait's freedom.

As in the past, Bush consulted just a few of his advisers before making the decision.[60] Scowcroft knew that Bush's diplomatic initiative was principally for show and that the president was determined to go to war.[61] Others outside the administration, however, questioned the decision. Kissinger warned that if a compromise was reached, it would signal that aggression was being rewarded. The Saudi ambassador complained that Saddam would interpret Bush's decision as an act of cowardice and would delay agreeing to meet with Baker until just before the UN deadline.[62]

Their concerns were justified. Baghdad, which for some time had argued that it was prepared to discuss the problem with U.S. representatives so long as the Bush administration did not impose preconditions, immediately exploited the offer. In early December, the Iraqi media stated, "The enemy of God, the arrogant President of the United States, George Bush, has consistently opposed dialogue . . . His initiative is [therefore] a submission to Iraq's demand, on which it has insisted and is still insisting . . ."[63] Washington and Baghdad spent much of December haggling over when to meet, with Saddam Hussein claiming that he could not meet until January 12, 1991. On January 3, Bush once again proposed that his secretary of state meet with Iraq's foreign minister. The meeting, which took place six days later, was a complete failure. After the talks ended, Baker told the international media that Iraq had not shown any flexibility "on complying with the United Nations Security Council resolutions." The secretary of state and his immediate advisers were convinced the Iraqi leadership believed that the United States lacked resolve largely because it still carried the baggage of Vietnam, and that the U.S. Congress and public were reluctant to become involved in another major war.[64]

Baker's conjecture was based, in part, on what had been ensuing in the United States. Concern about where the Congress would stand generated disagreement within the Bush administration. At the White House, Cheney argued that the Congress could not be trusted to support the president. On September 3, in front of the Senate Armed Services Committee, the secretary of defense stated: "I do not believe the president requires any additional authorization from Congress." Baker made a similar argument, in front of the same committee, a few days later. The president adhered to the same belief. "I still feel that I have the constitutional authority, many attorneys having so advised me." In private, Powell argued that it was imperative to have the Congress's backing.[65]

The Congress, however, was not yet prepared to surrender its authority. In early December, Democrats in the House of Representatives accused the president of rushing to war and warned that he could not go to war without Congressional approval. On December 27, 100 of them formally asked the president to give sanctions a chance. At the start of January, the disagreement between the White House and certain members of Congress became a mute issue. Speaker of the House Tom Foley announced that the House would address the matter regardless of whether the president requested congressional approval. Cognizant that it would be politically unwise not to send a request, the president did so on January 9, and congressional debate began the following day. Two days later the House voted 250 to 183, and the Senate 52 to 47, to authorize the president to use force against Iraq.[66] By then, more than 60 percent of the American public supported military action against Iraq. In the final analysis, however, maybe none of this really mattered. As explained by Gates, "Bush was going to throw the son of a bitch out of Kuwait whether or not Congress and public opinion supported him."[67] His assessment was right on target. Just before the end of the year, Bush remarked in private, "If I have to go [to war], it is not going to matter to me if there isn't one congressman who supports this, or what happens to public opinion. If it's right, it's gotta be done."[68]

During this period, the Pentagon continued to get ready for war. Near the end of December, Schwarzkopf informed Powell that he would be prepared to initiate the air campaign on the night of January 17. On December 29, Powell ordered Schwarzkopf to be set to initiate hostilities on the aforementioned date. In the meantime, intelligence analysts did not agree on whether Saddam Hussein would withdraw from Kuwait. The CIA and the Department of State argued that in view of the vastly superior strength of the coalition forces, it would be irrational for Saddam Hussein not to pull out. The DIA and the intelligence agencies from the four military services disagreed. They questioned the propensity of the CIA and the Department of State to project the Western approach to rationality on Saddam Hussein. For the challengers, the Iraqi leader's decision to invade Kuwait was a clear signal that he did not view the world in the same way some analysts in the United States thought he did. The *National Intelligence Estimate* (NIE), however, did not describe the divergence in estimates. It concluded that Saddam Hussein would yield, and included the opinions by DIA and military intelligence in only a few of its footnotes.[69] Some of the senior U.S. foreign policy-makers concurred with the NIE. Bush had great difficulty thinking that Saddam Hussein would not realize how costly it would be to him and his country to remain in Kuwait. It was not until late December that the president began to accept that his perception of the Iraqi leader might have been wrong. But by then all he could manage to ask was, "Is he crazy?" Powell remained convinced until the very end that Saddam Hussein was "rational" and would pull out of Kuwait.[70] On January 16 (17 in Kuwait and Iraq), as U.S. forces launched a series of attacks on Iraqi forces, those who believed that Saddam Hussein would retreat had no choice but to acknowledge that their prediction had been wrong.

To March or Not to March Toward Baghdad

On the morning of February 27, 1991, just 47 days after the campaign against Iraqi forces had been launched, Powell informed Bush and the other members of the senior decision-making group at the White House that the United States was "approaching the end game" and that he expected "that within the next twenty four hours—at [the] next meeting tomorrow morning—[he] would be bringing [the president] a recommendation with respect to the cessation of hostilities."[71] The news surprised Bush and Scowcroft. Psychologically unprepared, the president asked: "Well, if that's the case, we're within the window, why not end it now?"[72] With his principal objective attained, the president recognized that his promise to return Kuwait to its original leaders was about to be fulfilled.

Powell was pleased with the president's thinking. After discussing for a while longer with Bush and his other advisers the implications of stopping the war at that stage, the chairman of the Chiefs of Staff, accompanied by the secretary of defense, went to Congress to inform its leadership of the plan. Afterward, they addressed the matter with Schwarzkopf and the other members of the Chiefs of Staff. In the meantime, some of Bush's senior civilian foreign policy advisers contacted coalition members about the impending decision and began to write up the announcement. Later in the afternoon, Cheney and Powell returned to the White House to meet with the president. At the small gathering, which lasted only a brief while, Bush ordered that the war be ended. On February 28, 1991, at exactly 8:00 a.m. (G + 4), the war against Iraq came to a close.[73]

The Iraq War

Some war policies germinate in a short period; others take time to evolve. The decision by the Bush administration to use force to topple the Saddam regime belongs in the second category. The broad contours of the Bush administration's foreign policy toward Iraq saw their first light in 1992, when Secretary of Defense Cheney asked Wolfowitz, I. Lewis Libby, and Zalmay Khalilzad to draft a plan that would help reorient U.S. defense policy after the Cold War. In a document titled *Defense Planning Guidance* (DPG), the three Pentagon officials proposed a new post–Cold War era role for the United States. Because of the United States's vastly superior power, they argued, Washington had to commit itself to persuading its "potential competitors that they need not aspire to a greater role or pursue a more aggressive posture to protect their legitimate interests . . . [and must] discourage [potential competitors] from challenging [its] leadership or seeking to overturn the established political and economic order." They also emphasized that the United States "should be postured to act independently when collective action cannot be orchestrated."[74] This was the first time an administration advanced preemption and preventive war policies simultaneously. These ideas lost traction shortly after the document became public knowledge and Bush ordered Cheney to remove references to unilateral action, preemption, and prevention.[75]

The argument resurfaced with markedly more concrete goals several years later. In early January 1998, members of the *Project for the New American Century* proposed to President Bill Clinton that in his upcoming State of the Union Address he "chart a clear and determined course" aimed at the "removal of Saddam Hussein's regime from power . . . The policy of 'containment' of Saddam Hussein," they explained, "has been steadily eroding over the past few months . . . [o]ur ability to ensure that Saddam Hussein is not producing weapons of mass destruction . . . has substantially diminished . . . The only acceptable strategy is one that eliminates the possibility that Iraq will be able to use or threaten to use weapons of mass destruction. In the near term, this means a willingness to undertake military action as diplomacy is clearly failing. In the long term, it means removing Saddam Hussein and his regime from power. That needs now to become the aim of American foreign policy." Of the 18 individuals who signed the recommendation 11 would eventually become members of the Bush administration.[76]

Though the advice did not have the intended effect, Clinton began to intensify his anti-Saddam-Hussein stance. On February 17, during a visit to the Pentagon, the president stated that the "United States simply cannot allow Mr. Hussein to acquire nuclear, chemical and biological weapons arsenals." He added that it had to commit itself to fight "an unholy axis" of terrorists and "the outlaw nations" that harbor them.[77] Close to the end of the year, after the UN inspectors had decided to withdraw from Baghdad in protest of Saddam Hussein's obstructionist measures, Clinton informed the American people that he had "ordered America's Armed Forces to strike military and security targets in Iraq . . ." He went on to explain that Saddam Hussein's unwillingness to cooperate with the UN weapons inspectors, along with his earlier propensity to use WMD, presented "a clear and present danger to the stability of the Persian Gulf and the safety of people everywhere." Because of such a threat, the United States had no choice but to "pursue a long-term strategy to contain Iraq and its weapons of mass destruction, and work toward the day when Iraq has a government worthy of its people."[78]

By the start of the new millennium, and with the prospect of regaining the presidency, one of the Republican Party's rising stars added her voice to the call that the United States actively foster the overthrow of Saddam Hussein. In a widely publicized article published in early 2000, Condoleezza Rice, who had been advising presidential candidate George W. Bush on foreign policy matters, wrote: "Saddam Hussein's regime is isolated, his conventional military power has been severely weakened, his people live in poverty and terror, and he has no useful place in international politics. He is therefore determined to develop WMD. Nothing will change until Saddam is gone, so the United States must mobilize whatever resources it can, including support from his opposition, to remove him."[79] Four months after September 11, 2001, Rice, who by then was Bush's national security adviser, warned that by "both its actions and inactions, Iraq is proving not that it is a nation bent on disarmament, but that it is a nation with something to hide. Iraq is still treating inspections as a game. It should know that time is running out."[80] In early April 2002, the president, during a trip to England, did not mince words when he expressed his viewpoint about Saddam Hussein and WMD. "I made up my mind that Saddam needs to go." And he added, "The worst thing that could happen would be to allow a nation like Iraq, run by Saddam Hussein, to develop weapons of mass destruction, and then team up with terrorist organizations so they can blackmail the world. I'm not going to let that happen."[81] The subsequent month, as if to reiterate his boss's message, Secretary of Defense Rumsfeld made it quite clear that the "cause for war is the development of weapons of mass destruction by the Baghdad regime."[82] No one, however, made such a claim more emphatically than Cheney. In late August he stated: "There is no doubt that Saddam Hussein now has weapons of mass destruction [and] there is no doubt that he is amassing them to use against our friends, against our allies and against us."[83]

The rationale for war is rarely one-dimensional. Despite the weight placed on preventing Saddam Hussein from further developing and using Iraq's WMD, after the attacks on September 11 several members of the Bush administration underscored at least three other factors. For a few of its members, taking on Iraq was part of the

United States's worldwide strategy against terrorism—specifically against al Qaeda.

Establishing a link between al Qaeda and Saddam Hussein gradually became a compelling motivation—one that started to emerge earlier than September 11. In April 2001, during a meeting of the Deputies Committee, Richard Clarke who, as explained earlier, had served as the national coordinator for security and counterterrorism under the Clinton administration and would retain the post for several months under the new administration, proposed to its members that the United States "put pressure on both the Taliban and al Qaeda by arming the Northern Alliance and other groups in Afghanistan." Wolfowitz questioned Clarke's proposal. The deputy secretary of defense argued that Clarke was giving "bin Laden too much credit." Bin Laden, added Wolfowitz, "could not do all these things like the 1993 attack on New York without a state sponsor. Just because FBI and CIA have failed to find the linkages does not mean they don't exist."[84] Though at that time Wolfowitz did not state that bin Laden and Hussein were working together, he managed to plant the seeds for future conjectures. The September 11 attacks provided Wolfowitz an opening. Six days after the assaults, he wrote Rumsfeld a memo headlined "Preventing More Events." In it, the deputy secretary of defense argued that if there was even a 10 percent chance that Hussein had backed the attacks, the United States should give top priority to eliminating him.[85] By then, the president, who suspected that there was a link between Saddam Hussein and al Qaeda, had already ordered Clarke to investigate whether the two were connected.[86] The suspicion took on a more definitive tone later that year, when the vice president stated during a public appearance that it was "pretty well confirmed" that Mohamed Atta, the September 11 mastermind, had met with a senior Iraqi intelligence official before the attacks.[87] During the next 15 months, other members of the administration continued to reiterate the same message: al Qaeda and Saddam Hussein were connected. In 2002, Tenet wrote that the CIA had "solid reporting of senior level contacts between Iraq and al Qaeda going back a decade" and that "credible information [indicated] that Iraq and al Qaeda have discussed safe haven and reciprocal non-aggression."[88] In early January 2003, Bush, during his State of the Union address, stated that the evidence "from intelligence sources, secret communications and statements by people now in custody reveal that Saddam Hussein aids and protects terrorists, including members of al Qaeda." A few days later, Powell repeated Bush's assertion before the United Nations. "Iraq," said Powell, "today harbors a deadly terrorist network headed by Abu Mussab al-Zarqawi, a collaborator of Osama bin Laden and his al Qaeda lieutenants . . . When our coalition ousted the Taliban, al Zarqawi helped establish another poison and explosive training center camp. And this camp is located in northeastern Iraq." After describing other connections between al Qaeda and members of Saddam's regime, Powell explained why the Bush administration believed it was critical to take them seriously. "Some believe, some claim these contacts do not amount to much. They say Saddam Hussein's secular tyranny and al Qaeda's religious tyranny do not mix. I am not comforted by this thought. Ambition and hatred are enough to bring Iraq and al Qaeda together, enough so al Qaeda could learn how to build more sophisticated bombs and learn how to forge documents, and enough so that al Qaeda could turn to Iraq for help in acquiring expertise on weapons of mass destruction."[89]

The promotion of democracy in Iraq and in the surrounding areas was the Bush administration's third rationale. Were they to achieve this goal, reasoned some of its members, the United States would help stabilize the region and enhance Israel's security. The notion that the United States had a moral responsibility to promote democracy and that the spread of such a regime in a region and throughout the world would help generate stability preceded the Bush administration. In 1917, when President Woodrow Wilson went before a joint session of Congress to propose the United States enter a war that had engulfed Europe for nearly three years, he stated that their country had to take such a step "for democracy, for the right of those who submit to authority to have a choice in their own government . . . and to make the world itself at least free." Three-quarters of a century later, with communism no longer a threat, Americans were asked by President William Clinton to believe that for the United States there was no national interest "more urgent than securing democracy's triumph around the world." As explained by National Security Adviser Anthony Lake, the "successor to a doctrine of containment must be a strategy of enlargement—enlargement of the world's free community market democracies."[90]

The Bush administration concurred with its forerunner, but not necessarily with its predecessor's reliance on multilateral agreements and international norms. To help spawn new democracies, it was imperative to revitalize U.S. military power and pay closer attention to geopolitical relations. In Rice's own words, "peace is the first and most important condition for continued prosperity and freedom. America's military power must be secure because the United States is the only guarantor of global peace and security."[91]

In the Bush administration there was no one as committed as its leader to the idea that the United States had a moral obligation to propagate democratic values. For Bush, going to war against Iraq entailed much more than defeating an enemy. He wanted the United States to be viewed as a "liberator." In times of war, he explained, there "is a human condition that [one] must worry . . . There is a value system that cannot be compromised—God-given values. These aren't United States-created values. These are values of free-dom and the human condition and mothers loving their children. What's very important as [the United States] articulate[s] foreign policy through diplomacy and military action, is that it never look like [as if it were] creating . . . these values."[92] The president restated his vision during discussions with Rice and her deputy Stephen J. Hadley regarding what he should say at his upcoming January 2002 State of the Union speech. At one point, when Rice and Hadley wondered whether Bush should include Iran as part of the "axis of evil," the president said, "It is very important for the American pres-ident at this point in history to speak very clearly about the evils the world faces. No question about it, North Korea, Iraq and Iran are the biggest threats to peace at this time." He added, "I believe the United

States is the beacon for freedom in the world. And I believe we have a responsibility to promote freedom that is as solemn as the responsibility is to protecting the American people, because the two go hand-in-hand . . . [F]reedom is not America's gift to the world. Freedom is God's gift to everybody in the world . . . [W]e have a duty to free people. I would hope we wouldn't have to do it militarily, but we have a duty." Bush then demanded that the speech include language about promoting democratic and human rights values.[93]

This notion assumed an official role on August 14, 2002 when it became part of a National Security Presidential Directive. If the United States went to war against Iraq, it would do so, in part, to "liberate the Iraqi people from tyranny, and assist them in creating a society based on modernism, pluralism and democracy." The postwar intent would be to "establish a broad-based democratic government that would adhere to international law and respect international norms, and would not threaten its neighbors, that would respect the basic rights of all Iraqis, including women and minorities, that would adhere to the rule of law, including freedom of speech and worship." To achieve these ends, the United States and its allies would employ "all instruments of national power to free Iraq . . ." and a strategy that would require working "with the Iraqi opposition to demonstrate that we are liberating, not invading, Iraq, and give the opposition a role in building a pluralistic and democratic Iraq, including the preparation of a new constitution . . ."[94]

The fourth rationale, and one that the Bush administration, for obvious reasons, did not articulate with great frequency, was the United States's long-standing dependence on Persian Gulf oil. The overthrow of the Shah of Iran in 1979 by Islamic militants loyal to Ayatollah Khomeini compelled President Jimmy Carter to design a doctrine, which stated that the United States would employ whatever means might be necessary, "including military force," to ensure the continuing flow of oil from the Persian Gulf. When Iraq invaded Kuwait in 1990, the first Bush administration made it clear that the United States could not permit Hussein to control 20 percent of the world's oil reserves (Iraq's plus Kuwait's), much less 40 percent, which would happen if his forces also marched into Saudi Arabia. More than a decade later, and in possession of WMD, Iraq would be in a position to gain control over a large segment of the world's oil reserves. As explained by Cheney in August 2002, "Armed with these weapons of terror and a seat at the top of ten percent of the world's oil reserves, Saddam Hussein could then be expected to seek domination of the entire Middle East, take control of a great portion of the world's energy supplies, directly threaten America's friends throughout the region, and subject the United States or any other nation to nuclear blackmail."[95]

Because we lack the kind of information necessary to ascertain the weight the Bush administration placed on each rationale, we will avoid contending that some of its motives were more important and authentic than others. For present purposes, such differentiation is not critical. Of markedly greater significance is the quality and quantity of the intelligence relied on by the Bush administration to conceive its first three rationales.[96]

The Role of Intelligence

Every member of any intelligence community and every foreign policy-maker knows that intelligence is not a fact but a judgment derived from information that is often incomplete and unreliable. When faced with an international challenge, the foreign policy-maker is sometimes forced to find a balance between the amount of information he needs in order to formulate a policy and the costs that he might spawn if he delays his decision until he has collected additional and better intelligence. For instance, if a foreign policy-maker suspects that an adversary is developing WMD but does not have enough evidence to substantiate his fear, he faces a dilemma. He must decide whether to risk being wrong and take action against his adversary without sufficient intelligence, or continue collecting more intelligence, thus giving his opponent additional time to develop WMD. This was the dilemma the Bush administration believed it faced in 2002.

In early 2001, just as Bush was assuming the presidency, U.S. intelligence agencies learned that Iraq wanted to buy 60,000 high-strength aluminum tubes from Hong Kong. The tubes, made of an extremely strong alloy, could potentially be used as rotors in uranium centrifuges.[97] A few months later, on April 10, a division within the CIA, known as Weapons Intelligence, Nonproliferation and Arms Control (Winpac), reported that the tubes "have little use other than uranium enrichment program." Not everyone in the intelligence community agreed with the CIA's assessment. The Department of Energy argued that the tubes were too long, too narrow, and too heavy to be used in a centrifuge.[98] Shortly afterward, it added that the tubes could be used to make combustion chambers for slim rockets fired from launcher pods, just as Iraq had done in the mid-1990s, and that the International Atomic Energy Agency (IAEA) had reached a similar conclusion. IAEA, in fact, had reported that the measurements of the aluminum tubes matched exactly the dimensions of the ones Iraq had been attempting to purchase.

The disagreement continued even after a shipment of tubes going to Iraq was seized in Jordan in June. Scientists at the Department of Energy examined them, and reported their findings on August 7. Despite the fact that they questioned the suitability of the tubes for centrifuges, they were not ready to forward an unambiguous conclusion. Using the aluminum tubes in centrifuges, they argued, "is credible but unlikely . . . a rocket production is the much more likely end use for these tubes." British experts and U.S. Department of State analysts concurred. In an attempt to erase some of the vagueness produced by its earlier report, the Department of Energy released a classified account at the end of 2001 arguing that in order to make one single nuclear bomb a year, Iraq would need to surmount an extraordinary technical challenge—the working in concert of some 16,000 tubes. Until then, they added, Iraq had never managed to make more than a dozen centrifuge prototypes. In March 2002, Cheney read a report put together by the DIA, which stated that Iraq had attempted to buy 500 tons of yellowcake, a uranium concentrate, from Niger. He and other senior administration officials also learned from two CIA reports that Iraq "may be trying to reconstitute its gas centrifuge program." The reports did not disclose that the Department of Energy disagreed with that conclusion, but the difference in interpretation seemed to have been explained by CIA officials during private conversations with senior members of the Bush administration.

Exposure of the differences seemed to have little effect on senior administrators, especially Cheney, Rice, and Bush. During an address to the Veterans of Foreign Wars national convention in August 2002, the vice president stated: "Many of us are convinced that Saddam will acquire nuclear weapons fairly soon. Just how soon, we cannot really gauge. Intelligence is an uncertain business, even in the best of circumstances." He then warned that the United States could not afford to engage in "wishful thinking or willful blindness."[99] To support his contention, the vice president cited information provided by Saddam Hussein's son-in-law, Hussein Kamel al-Majid, who, prior to defecting in 1994, had run Iraq's chemical, biological, and nuclear weapons program. There were two problems with Cheney's claim. First, Saddam Hussein's son-in-law had stated, when interrogated by U.S. military intelligence in 1995, that Iraq had dismantled its nuclear program. And second, he was assassinated in 1996 after returning to Iraq, thus making it impossible for him to know what Saddam Hussein was doing in 2001.

The following month, during a *Meet the Press* interview, Cheney sought to explain the amount of information he and others in the administration had access to, and the kinds of inferences they were deriving. He acknowledged that the Bush administration did not "have all the evidence. We have 10 percent, 20 percent, 30 percent. We don't know how much. We know we have part of the picture." But he then added: "[T]hat part of the picture tells us that he is, in fact, actively and aggressively seeking to acquire nuclear weapons."[100] Possibly concerned that his words might have created some doubt, he stated: "He [Saddam Hussein] has reconstituted his nuclear program." He expressed his conviction once again in front of a group of Wyoming Republicans when he told them the administration had "irrefutable evidence" that Saddam Hussein was rebuilding Iraq's nuclear weapons program.[101] The national security adviser voiced the same message. During a CNN interview conducted on September 8, Rice disregarded the disagreements within the intelligence community with the contention that the high-strength aluminum tubes were "only really suited for nuclear weapons program." As if to ensure that no one would question her claim, she then warned that the United States did not want "the smoking gun to be a mushroom cloud."[102] Four days later, the president made a similar argument at the United Nations. "Iraq," Bush stated, "has made several attempts to buy high-strength aluminum tubes used in centrifuges to enrich uranium for a nuclear weapon."[103] Though senior CIA officials had been asked by the White House to review this sentence and others before the president delivered the speech, they did not propose any changes. Specifically, they did not warn that the tubes could be used for a purpose other than the one put forward by the president, and that many U.S. military intelligence experts disagreed with the claim made in the sentence. Despite the CIA's failure to point out the aforesaid discrepancy, the White House was well aware that it existed.

The CIA ceded some ground later in September. In a detailed report to the policy-makers, it acknowledged that some members in the intelligence community believed that Iraq intended to use the tubes to build rockets. In the meantime, the Department of Energy asked the Institute for Science and International Security to review the analyses of the tube and derive its own conclusion. The Institute sided with the Department of Energy's argument. Also during this period, Democratic senators demanded the issuing of a National Intelligence Estimate on Iraq—a document designed to reflect the combined judgment of the entire intelligence community. And yet, shortly afterward, the Department of Energy decided to concur with the CIA's major contention. It stated that despite the fact that it did not believe the tubes would be used for centrifuges, it agreed with the CIA when it said Iraq was reconstituting its nuclear weapons program. It based its conclusion, principally, on the suspicion that

Iraq was trying to buy yellowcake uranium from Niger. Neither the Department of State nor the CIA considered the intelligence on such matters reliable.

The authors of the National Intelligence Estimate took advantage of the Department of Energy's latest conjecture to argue that the latter and the CIA concurred that Saddam Hussein was rebuilding its nuclear program.[104] They noted they had "moderate confidence" that "Iraq does not yet have a nuclear weapon or sufficient material to make one but is likely to have a weapon by 2007 to 2009."[105] They relegated statements by dissenters to a ten-page appendix. On October 2, nine days before the Senate voted on the war resolution, its Intelligence Committee received the estimate. A few days later, during a visit to Connecticut, the president stated that the United States could not afford "to wait for the final proof—the smoking gun—that could come in the form of a mushroom cloud." On October 11, the Senate gave Bush the authority he had asked for by a 77 to 23 vote.

The vote did not annul discord between the different organizations. Not long after Iraq had submitted its declaration about unconventional arms to the United Nations, the CIA criticized it for not acknowledging or explaining why Saddam Hussein's regime had attempted to acquire tubes "suitable for use in a gas centrifuge uranium effort" and "to procure uranium from Niger." The criticism was composed without any input from either the Department of State or the Department of Energy. By then, however, inspectors from IAEA had started to inspect the famed aluminum tubes. Moreover, by the second week of January 2003, the IAEA had concluded that there was no evidence to prove Iraq had a clandestine centrifuge program. Fearful that its justification for war against Saddam Hussein might be eroding, the Bush administration redoubled its effort to prove it was the Iraqi leader's intent to set up a nuclear program. It did not succeed. And yet, this had little effect on the president. On January 27, the day before Bush stated during his State of the Union address that Saddam Hussein was trying to buy aluminum tubes "suitable for nuclear weapons production," the IAEA informed the United Nations Security Council that analysis indicated the aluminum tubes inspected in Iraq "would be consistent with the purpose stated by Iraq [to improve its rocket's accuracy and avert corrosion] and, unless modified, would not be suitable for manufacturing centrifuges." The IAEA's director Mohamed ElBaradei summarized the agency's findings as follows: "We have to date found no evidence that Iraq has revived its nuclear weapons program since its elimination of the program in the 1990s." He added, "We should be able within the next few months to provide credible assurance that Iraq has no nuclear program."[106] A senior administration official who helped vet the president's speech explained the discrepancy in interpretation by noting that the IAEA had examined the old aluminum tubes but not the new one seized in Iraq. The IAEA refuted the assertion with the contention that it examined both.

By February 5, the day Powell was scheduled to go before the Security Council to present the United States's case for war against Iraq, there was little reason to think that the secretary of state would challenge the administration's version, despite the fact that the intelligence community did not speak with one voice. In response to circulated drafts of his speech, intelligence analysts at the Department of State made it clear that the language regarding the aluminum tubes included "egregious errors" and "highly misleading" declarations. They went so far as to point out that "the U.S. Mark 66 air-launched 70-milliliter rocket . . . uses the same high grade (7075-T6) aluminum, and . . . has specifications with similar tolerances." But to no avail. In front of the UN Security Council, Powell said, "[T]here is no doubt in my mind these illicit procurement efforts show that Saddam Hussein is very much focused on putting in place the key missing piece from his nuclear weapons program: the ability to produce fissile material."[107]

In short, the Bush administration's claim that Iraq was developing WMD was not grounded in "current intelligence that . . . is very convincing," as Wolfowitz had asserted.[108] Intelligence analysts had limited information and lacked up-to-date intelligence. As explained by Richard Kerr, a former CIA deputy director, intelligence analysts "drew heavily on a base of hard evidence growing out of the lead-up to the first war, the first war itself and then the inspection process. We had a rich base of information," and after the inspectors left Iraq in 1998, "we drew on that earlier base. There were pieces of new information, but not a lot of hard information, and so the products that dealt with WMD were based heavily on analysis drawn out of that earlier period."[109] The Commission on the Intelligence Capabilities of the United States Regarding Weapons of Mass Destruction established by President Bush concurs with the last assessment. Because of the lack of solid information, the U.S. intelligence community was forced to fall back on "inferences drawn from Iraq's past behavior and intentions." After the end of the 1991 Gulf War, it realized that it had badly underestimated Iraq's weapons of mass destruction capabilities and was "determined not to fall victim again of the same mistake." Thus, it assumed throughout the 1990s that Baghdad had maintained its WMD capabilities and augmented them after Saddam Hussein had forced the weapons inspectors to leave Iraq.[110]

In view of the fact that the Bush administration did not possess sound information that proved Iraq was close to developing a nuclear weapon, the next task is to ascertain whether the asserted linkage between Saddam Hussein and al Qaeda was backed by more reliable intelligence. It may not be possible to identify at this time the originator of the idea that Saddam Hussein and al Qaeda were connected, but it is fair to speculate that Rumsfeld's deputy secretary played a central role. As may be recalled, Wolfowitz planted the first seed during a meeting of the Deputies Committee in April 2001, at which time he challenged Clarke's contention that the United States needed "to put pressure on both the Taliban and al Qaeda by arming the Northern Alliance and other groups in Afghanistan." Bin Laden, argued Wolfowitz, "could not do all these things like the 1993 attack on New York without a state sponsor. Just because FBI and CIA have failed to find the linkages does not mean they don't exist."[111] Clarke's response was blunt. "I am unaware," he stated, "of any Iraqi-sponsored terrorism directed at the United States, and I think FBI and CIA concur in that judgment . . ." The CIA deputy director John McLaughlin agreed with Clarke. "We have no evidence of any active Iraqi terrorist threat against the U.S."[112] Though at that point Wolfowitz was merely suggesting that bin Laden could not be particularly effective without the support of a rogue state, he was markedly more forceful after September 11. As already noted, six days after the attacks, he wrote Rumsfeld that if there was even a ten percent chance Hussein had backed the attacks, the United States should give top priority to eliminating him.[113]

The drive to link Saddam Hussein with al Qaeda continued to intensify, but the answers from the experts did not change. In response to a request by Bush that he investigate whether there was a link between al Qaeda and Iraq, Clarke sent the president a memo assuring him that the agencies and departments agreed "there was no cooperation between the two."[114] In February 2002, a classified DIA report questioned the notion that Iraq and al Qaeda were working together based on the recognition that the person who had initially made the claim might have been subjected to harsh treatment while a prisoner in Egypt.[115] In the early summer, the CIA noted in a document titled "Iraq and al Qaida: Interpreting a Murky Relationship" that "many critical gaps" existed in the knowledge of Iraqi links to al Qaeda because of "limited reporting and the questionable reliability of many of our sources."[116] In August, former national security adviser Brent Scowcroft, who had retained his contacts in the intelligence community, wrote in an article published by *The Wall Street Journal*: "[T]here is scant evidence to tie Saddam to terrorist organizations, and even less to the Sept. 11 attacks. Indeed Saddam's goals have little in common with the terrorists who threaten us, and there is little incentive to make common cause with them. He is unlikely to risk his investment in weapons of mass destruction, much less his country, by handing such weapons to terrorists who would use them for their own purposes and leave Baghdad as the return address. Threatening to use these weapons for blackmail—much less their actual use—would open him and his entire regime to a devastating response by the U.S. While Saddam is thoroughly evil, he is above all a power-hungry survivor."[117]

The National Intelligence Council presented a nuanced assessment in its 92-page National Intelligence Estimate. It contended that Saddam Hussein, "if sufficiently desperate, might decide that only an organization such as al Qaeda—with worldwide reach and extensive terrorist infrastructure, and already engaged in a life-or-death struggle against the United States—would perpetrate the type of terrorist attack that he would hope to conduct. In such circumstances, he might decide that the extreme step of assisting the Islamist terrorists in conducting a CBW attack against the United States would be his last chance to exact vengeance by taking a large number of victims with him." The Council, however, did acknowledge that it had "low confidence" in its assessment and that the agencies did not "have any specific intelligence information that Saddam's regime has directed attacks against U.S. territory."[118] Powell conceded as much when, as he prepared for his presentation to the United Nations Security Council in early 2003, he complained that the intelligence linking Saddam Hussein to al Qaeda was not particularly strong. Tenet, who was in the best position to know whether the intelligence was reliable, made it clear to senior members of the Bush administration that there was no proof of Iraq running terrorist groups. The most he could claim was that, technically, the Iraqi regime was harboring terrorists. The CIA director built his argument on the contention that a Palestinian named Abu Musab al-Zarqawi, with strong al Qaeda ties, was operating a training center in northern Iraq. Military intelligence, wrote Tenet, had "solid reporting of senior level contacts between Iraq and al Qaeda going back a decade . . ." He also stated that the CIA had "credible information [indicating] that Iraq and al Qaeda have discussed safe haven and reciprocal non-aggression."[119]

There are several major inconsistencies in Tenet's assertions. First, they do not take into account the fact that the CIA already knew bin Laden had "been sponsoring anti-Saddam Islamists in Iraqi Kurdistan, and sought to attract them into his Islamic army." Eventually bin Laden agreed to stop supporting anti-Saddam activities, but he continued to "aid a group of Islamist extremists operating in part of Iraq (Kurdistan) outside Baghdad's control."[120] A second inconsistency involved two CIA memoranda, which stated that the chief of Iraq's intelligence and expert in bomb making met with bin Laden at his farm outside Khartoum, Sudan, on July 30, 1996, and stayed in the area giving training until September 1996. This statement was "puzzling since bin Laden left Sudan for Afghanistan in May 1996, and there [was] no evidence he ventured back there (or anywhere else) for a visit."[121] Third, though it was true that bin Laden and Iraq intermittently sought to develop a better relationship, for a variety of reasons they never formalized an agreement. Fourth, by the time Bush had decided to order the invasion of Iraq, U.S. military intelligence had confirmed that al Qaeda had established ties with Iran and Hezbollah. And fifth, despite repeated claims that the mastermind of the September 11 attacks, Mohamed Atta, had met with a senior Iraqi intelligence official in Prague before that ill-fated date, the CIA had enough intelligence to dismiss such an inference.[122] In short, it is justifiable to conclude that before Bush ordered the invasion of Iraq, U.S. intelligence agencies did not have credible evidence indicating the Saddam Hussein regime "cooperated with al Qaeda in developing or carrying out attacks against the United States."[123] Or, as noted by Paul R. Pillar, the national intelligence officer for the Near East and South Asia at the CIA from 2000 to 2005, the intelligence gathering process expected by the Bush administration was not "designed to find dangers not yet discovered or to inform decisions not yet made. Instead, it involved research to find evidence in support of a specific line of argument—that Saddam was cooperating with al Qaeda—which in turn was being used to justify a specific policy decision."[124]

Trying to link the Bush administration's third rationale to available intelligence is a markedly more cumbersome analytical task. Foreign policy entails more than identifying an objective. It requires the design of a strategy that delineates the interconnection between an objective and a policy. For the third rationale—the promotion of democracy in Iraq and the surrounding areas—to be properly connected to a policy, U.S. military intelligence had to possess knowledge about Iraq's past and existing political, economic, and social conditions. It also needed to understand the kind of obstacles the United States would encounter as it sought to set up the foundations of a democratic regime following the removal of the Saddam Hussein regime, and what it would have to do in order to overcome them. Moreover, to determine the means it would have to employ to surmount the impediments it would most likely encounter in Iraq, the Bush administration would have had to rely on knowledge the United States had gathered from its previous attempts to transform nondemocratic states into democratic ones. This type of knowledge was abundant and unambiguous.

What it takes to generate and preserve a stable democracy is an extensively studied subject. First, it is generally agreed that "democracy" refers to a system of government that enables substantial competition among individuals and political parties for governmental power at regularly scheduled intervals and without the use of force; extensive political participation from all adult social groups in the selection of leaders and policies; and enough civil liberties to protect the integrity of political competition and participation.[125] Second, it is commonly accepted that the creation of a democratic state typically can be divided into four phases. The initial state-building process entails the political, economic, and cultural unification of its elite. During this period "a series of bargains are struck and a variety of cultural bonds are established across networks of local power-holders and a number of institutions are built for the extraction of resources for common defense, for the maintenance of internal order and the adjudication of disputes, for the protection of established rights and privileges and for the elementary infrastructure require-ments of the economy and the polity." During the second phase, the center creates new channels of contact with the peripheries in order to induce the population to identify more closely with the political system. In the third phase, there is an increase in the level of partici-pation of the masses. This increase takes place through the granting of rights to the opposition, the creation of political parties, and the extension of the electorate. In the final phase, the state experiences a growth in the agencies of redistribution.[126]

Third, it is widely acknowledged that political legitimacy lies at the heart of all stable democracies. Political leaders, parties, social organizations, and the general public within a state are committed to democracy and to its rules and restraints, and reject any other possible type of political regime. This is the core condition for the consolidation of democracy.[127] The question at this juncture, thus, is: what are the conditions that facilitate and obstruct the development of a stable democracy? A newly created state's opportunity to grow into a stable and developed democratic entity in a world where the exercise of power is the defining practice depends largely on the ability of its domestic leaders to mitigate their political and economic differences, on its degree of ethnic, racial, religious, language, and class uniformity, and on the intensity of the external threats.

For starters, democracy cannot be formed without the presence of an effective state, and it will be derailed by the presence of exceptionally domineering state institutions.[128] During the state-building process, local power-holders must forge political agreements and build institutions capable of extracting resources for common defense, maintaining internal order and adjudicating disputes, protecting established rights and privileges, and creating the elementary economic and political infrastructures. Cooperation ensues when rivals adjust their behavior to the actual or anticipated preference of each other[129]—the greater the distances between the actual or anticipated preferences of two or more rivals, the smaller the likelihood that they will cooperate.[130] And, as suggested earlier, social, economic, religious, racial, ethnic, and language cleavages can affect the distances.

For a state to be democratic, a government of civilians must control the state security apparatus. Specifically, they must have the power to define the military apparatus's goals and supervise the organization and implementation of the state's defense. In today's democracies, political parties are the definers of political competition. Democracies without strong and cohesive parties and party systems are typically encroached by authoritarian leaders and military coups. Strong political parties that rely on deeply seated ideological pleas to garner public support, however, often generate excessive sectarianism and polarization that can, in turn, spawn intense instability. Their actions will be especially divisive when the state is afflicted by deep social, economic, ethnic, racial, language, and religious cleavages.

During their early stages, democracies are greatly dependent on leadership. The early leaders of a democracy must be individuals who will not be tempted to exploit their success in order to impose themselves as dictators, possess the ability to adjust and enlarge the political system in order to satisfy expanding demands for participation, and have the flexibility and astuteness to respond rapidly and effectively to political and economic crises. Effective leadership, however, is not enough. Ultimately, a stable democracy will emerge only if it develops a pluralistic and autonomous civil society capable of limiting the power of the state and expressing democratically its broad range of interests.[131]

Fourth, it is usually conceded that despite its repeated attempts to transform nondemocratic regimes into democratic ones, the United States's record has been less than stellar. Nowhere has the United States been more determined to foster the creation of democratic regimes than in its own "backyard"—Latin America. But as noted by a distinguished scholar, the U.S. drive to export democracy from the time of Woodrow Wilson to the present "has only rarely had a positive and lasting impact . . ."[132] Other conclusions that have been derived from analyses of U.S. attempts to spawn democratic regimes throughout Latin America are:

1. The "more interventionist the United States has been in Latin America—contravening sovereignty and overwhelming local actors— the less it has been able to foster lasting democratic politics . . ."

2. It "is easier for the United States to help protect democracy under siege than to implant democratic practices where they have not been previously rooted."

3. "The capacity of the U.S. government to nurture democratic politics in Latin America is greatest in those countries where the United States is sufficiently involved to be influential but

not so extensively engaged as to warp the domestic fabric of social and political life. Even in such nations, the United States is only likely to be effective in promoting democracy when U.S. influence is consistently exerted."

4. "External factors, including U.S. policy, are usually of secondary or tertiary importance in determining a Latin American nation's prospect for democracy . . ."[133]

The knowledge acquired by the United States during its repeated attempts to give rise to stable democracies throughout various parts of Latin America has to be compared with its experiences elsewhere. The U.S. efforts in the Philippines took about eight decades to germinate, and it is still unclear whether they will ultimately bear the sought-out fruit. Its labors in Vietnam have led to naught. On the other hand, the United States's promotion of democracy after World War II has paid off in France, Italy, South Korea, West Germany, and Japan.[134] Hence the question: which are the relevant analogies?

France and Italy are not germane analogies for obvious reasons. The United States intervened to free France from German control during World War II; the task of rebuilding France's democratic institutions, however, fell almost entirely on the shoulders of its leaders and people. Italy's experience did not differ significantly from France's. Though an ally of Germany during part of World War II, the overthrow of Benito Mussolini in 1943, prior to Germany's defeat, reduced markedly the United States's need to retain forces in the country. The Italians, like the French, assumed most of the burden of rebuilding their democratic institutions. South Korea is also an inapplicable case, but for a different reason. Despite the intense and extensive involvement of the United States in South Korea during and after the end of the Korean War, Washington waited more than three decades before demanding that South Korea abandon its nondemocratic past. During the interim period, the United States turned a blind eye to Seoul's authoritarian political practices although it provided the security and financial assistance South Korea needed in order to build and solidify its domestic economic system. This leaves Japan and West Germany as possible suitable analogies.

In order to ascertain whether it is appropriate to use Japan and West Germany as analogies, first it is necessary to delineate Iraq's political, economic, and social contours. Before Iraq was Iraq, the Ottomans ruled it. The British supplanted the Ottomans as Iraq's rulers during World War I. The first major challenge the British faced was the integration of a region with a population that was 75 percent tribal and was splintered along regional, ethnic, linguistic, and religious lines. The Kurds, a scattered tribal people who are mostly Sunni Muslims, who speak a language of the Iranian groups, and who are thought to be of Indo-European descent, inhabit the plateaus and mountains of northern Iraq.[135] Since Iraq's conception as a state, the Kurds have engendered the most unrelenting and effective threat to its security. Their last major, but unsuccessful, drive for autonomy prior to 2003 came shortly after the United States and its allies expelled the Iraqi troops from Kuwait in early 1991. In the Arab world the Sunnis vastly outnumber the Shiites, but in Iraq they constitute a minority. Though Shiites and Sunnis pray to the same god, revere the same prophet, and read the same holy book, in Iraq they have not shared power proportionally. During World War I, when the British supplanted the Ottomans as Iraq's new rulers, they brought from the outside a member of the Sunni Hashemite family to rule the country. The Sunnis dominated Iraq's political arena until 1968 when the Baath Party seized power completely. The change in regime dissipated some of the power imbalance. In spite of the fact that during his rule Saddam Hussein favored the Sunnis and repressed the Shiites in a manner markedly more forceful than any of his forerunners, many Shiites managed to prosper in Iraq's political, military, and economic arenas. Notwithstanding these positive developments, the Shiites have been waiting to play their "rightful role in Iraq," in the words of a cleric in Najaf, "since the death of Imam Hussein—some 1,300 years ago."[136]

Japan is not an appropriate analogy for several reasons. First, when Japan conceded defeat in 1945 it did so unconditionally, and Emperor

Hirohito, who by tradition was associated with the sun and revered by the Japanese as a demigod, personally endorsed the surrender.[137] The emperor's approval enabled the leader of the invading forces, General Douglas MacArthur, to rule by fiat and to expect substantial acquiescence from the Japanese. Saddam Hussein never achieved the status held by the Japanese emperor, and no one in the Bush administration expected him to respond to defeat in the same manner Hirohito did.

Second, in the case of Japan, MacArthur was able to rely on its administrative infrastructure to launch political, economic, and social reforms. Because of the tremendous internal and external animosity they generated, the institutions put in place by Saddam Hussein's Baathist regime would most likely not survive his political demise. Third, while Japan was and remains a highly homogeneous society, Iraq, as explained earlier, has been troubled by deep cleavages. From knowledge accumulated through years of studying similar entities, it would have been reasonable to infer that were Saddam Hussein and his regime to be toppled, those determined to build a stable democratic state in Iraq would have to cope with its traditional regional, ethnic, religious, and tribal animosities. These hostilities would most likely spawn civil conflict between Sunnis and Shiites, especially in the Mesopotamian plain. And fourth, Japan did not possess extensive natural resources and did not share land borders with powerful neighbors. Iraq, on the other hand, controls the world's second largest oil deposits and is bordered by six meddling neighbors, each with its own distinct set of power interests.[138]

West Germany is also an unsuitable analogy. First, by the end of a war that had lasted some five years, West Germans had been thoroughly defeated and no longer possessed the material means and will to continue fighting. During the period that the United States was involved in the war, President Franklin Roosevelt opposed differentiating between the offensive regime of the enemy state and the civilian population that it had ruled.[139] President Bush, on the other hand, during the months and days preceding the war, distinguished between the Iraqi regime and the people it ruled and ordered the design of a war plan that would limit the costs inflicted on the population at large. Though one of Bush's intents was to minimize the extent to which the Iraqis would be alienated by the actions of the invading forces, the strategy would also provide those who did not welcome the "liberators" the opportunity to use violence to vent their discontent during the occupation period. Second, though in the case of Western Germany the United States could not rely on the authority of an emperor to govern and impose new sets of rules, it had the advantage of being able to share its occupation tasks with two other major powers—Great Britain and France.[140] In Iraq, U.S. military and civilian personnel would shoulder most of the responsibility. Third, notwithstanding the fact that both Adolf Hitler and Saddam Hussein imposed on their respective states rigid hierarchical systems and neither tolerated any form of dissent, only Germans had had the chance to experiment with democracy. Between 1871 and 1918, the Germans were ruled by a system that was little more than a façade of a parliamentary monarchy; after the kaiser was compelled to go into exile in 1918, however, they were forced to create a representative government. Their new system of government remained in place until Hitler obliterated it in the first half of the 1930s. And fourth, despite some religious and regional differences during their drive to put in place a democratic regime, the Germans never had to address the deep regional, linguistic, religious, ethnic, and language cleavages that would most likely affect Iraqis during their own attempt in the post-invasion period.

The information presented here is part of the government and public domain. Any political leader or analyst could have gathered it easily, and after a thoughtful and careful analysis would have had little choice but to infer that bringing democracy to Iraq would be a formidable, if not impossible, task. A CIA intelligence analyst considered such a task so demanding that he stated, "only a dunce or a man ready to be silent to protect his career could have failed to know the U.S.-led occupation of Iraq would create a 'mujahideen magnet' more powerful than Moscow created in Afghanistan."[141]

Two more measured assessments came from the National Intelligence Council and the U.S. Army War College. The National

Intelligence Council issued a report titled "Principal Challenges in Post-Saddam Iraq," in January 2003. Although the report did not stress the possibility of insurgency, it noted that the "building of an Iraqi democracy would be a long, difficult, and probably turbulent process, with potential for backsliding into Iraq's tradition of authoritarianism. Iraqi political culture does not foster liberalism or democracy. Iraq lacks the experience of a loyal opposition and effective institutions for mass political participation."[142] A month later, two faculty members at the U.S. Army War College, Conrad C. Crane and W. Andrew Terrill, contended that the United States must be ready to "occupy Iraq for an extended period of time following Saddam's defeat." In their analysis they included a series of warnings. First, they remarked, "[M]ost Iraqis and most Arabs will probably assume that the United States intervened in Iraq for its own reasons and not to liberate the population." "Occupation problems," they added, "may be especially acute if the United States must implement the bulk of the occupation itself rather than turn these duties over to a postwar international force . . . [T]he Arab world today is extraordinarily sensitive to the question of Western domination and has painful memories of imperialism." After enumerating the various obstacles the United States would most likely encounter, the authors explained that the "establishment of democracy or even some sort of rough pluralism in Iraq, where it has never really existed previously, will be a staggering challenge for any occupation force seeking to govern in a post-Saddam era. Essentially, such a force must support changes in the fundamental character of the Iraqi political system, where anti-democratic traditions are deeply ingrained as they are throughout the wider Arab world."[143]

The concerns underlined by the National Intelligence Council and by members of the U.S. Army War College were shared by some of Bush's senior advisers. As chairman of the Joint Chiefs of Staff in 1992, Powell revisited the first Bush administration's decision not to march into Baghdad by asking: "How might the situation that we seek to alter, once it is altered by force, develop further and what might be the consequences?" After noting that the purpose of invading Iraq would have been to topple the Saddam Hussein regime, he wondered: "Would it have been worth the inevitable follow-up: Major occupation forces in Iraq for years to come and a very expensive and complex American pro-consulship in Baghdad?" His answer: "Fortunately for America, reasonable people at the time thought not."[144] Years later, as secretary of state, Powell voiced the same concern to the younger Bush. During a private meeting at the White House in August 5, 2002, the secretary of state warned the president that he "will become the government until you get a government. You are going to be the proud owner of 25 million people. You will own their hopes, aspirations and problems. You'll own it all." After stressing that Iraq had had a very complex history, one that had never included democracy, Powell remarked: "[Y]ou need to understand that this is not going to be a walk in the woods."[145] Even the secretary of defense, who was one of the earliest advocates of toppling the Saddam Hussein regime, feared that following the invasion "Iraq could experience ethnic strife among the Sunnis, Shiites and Kurds as has happened before."[146] But it was Haass, the director of planning under Powell at the Department of State during the war-planning period, who best encapsulated how difficult it would be for the United States to create a democracy in Iraq. "There's probably no harder foreign policy task than to get inside another society and try to help shape its politics and its economics . . . Democracy has to largely be homegrown . . . We can help make sure that democracy has a chance to root. But ultimately, it's going to really depend upon the society in question, the political leadership of that society, the business leadership of that society . . ."[147]

Many analysts outside the U.S. government expressed similar trepidations. Shibley Telhami, a highly regarded expert on the Middle East, warned in an article in *The Middle East Journal* published in 2002: "I don't think that U.S. policy right now can be oriented at 'winning hearts and minds' of the Middle East in the short term. That is not going to happen. The U.S. has a legacy of decades that is based in part on our policy and in part on impression; it is not going to be able to change the paradigm overnight simply by a charm campaign . . . People are not going to trust the message if they don't trust the messenger."[148] Stephen Walt, a Harvard professor, was no less doubtful. Iraq, he said, is "a country driven with internal divisions. That's why the Bush people didn't go to Baghdad in 1991 . . . I have limited confidence in our ability to run countries we don't understand . . . We've seen people attempting this in the Middle East before, and it hasn't worked. You never know how these operations will go. History is not on the side of the advocates here."[149] Pat Buchanan, a renowned conservative voice, echoed these concerns. "Anyone who believes America can finish Saddam and go home," he observed, "deceives himself. With Iraq's military crushed, the country will come apart . . . U.S. troops will have to remain to hold Iraq together, to find and destroy those weapons, to democratize the regime, and to deter Iran from biting off a chunk and dominating the Gulf . . . With Iraq in ruins, America will have to assume the permanent role of Policeman of the Persian Gulf."[150]

Many also wondered whether the United States would have enough troops to stabilize and democratize Iraq after the removal of the Saddam Hussein regime. In early January 2003, the former chairman of the Joint Chiefs of Staff, General Hugh Shelton, in a meeting at the Pentagon, cautioned "that the United States would not have sufficient troops immediately after the dictator was ousted." His counsel was based on information he had received from his various contacts in the Middle East who "warned that Iraq could devolve into chaos after Mr. Hussein was deposed."[151] James A. Dobbins, who had served as the ambassador at large for Kosovo, Bosnia, Somalia, and Haiti and was the administration's special envoy to Afghanistan, believed that the Yugoslavia model, with its deep ethnic divisions, was a better model than Afghanistan.[152] Even strong advocates of the war such as Robert Kagan and William Kristol, who for years had called for toppling the Saddam Hussein regime, voiced alarm. "The best way to avoid chaos and anarchy in Iraq after Saddam is removed," wrote Kagan and Kristol some two months before the war started, "is to have a powerful American occupying force in place, with the clear intention of sticking around for a while. We have already begun to see the price of not having such a force in Afghanistan. In Iraq, even more than in Afghanistan, the task of nation-building will be crucial. We don't want a vacuum power in Iraq."[153] Newt Gingrich, a former Speaker of the House, an adviser to the Pentagon, and a strong advocate of using the U.S. military power to transform Iraq, also feared that Rumsfeld and his advisers were underestimating what it would be needed in order to defeat Saddam Hussein and instill order in his country. In early February 2003, he warned that there was, "a mind-set arrogance compounded by what they saw in Afghanistan that has led people to think that 3 JDAMs [Joint Direct Attack Munition, a satellite guided bomb] and five guys on horseback equal a RG [Republican Guard] division."[154] Ultimately, however, none of the warnings convinced Bush that he needed to reassess his overall policy. In fact, on March 6, 2003, less than two weeks before he ordered the attack on Iraq, Bush dismissed the arguments advanced by those who questioned his optimism.

> There was a time when many said that the cultures of Japan and Germany were incapable of sustaining democratic values. Well they were wrong. Some say the same of Iraq today. They are mistaken. The nation of Iraq, with its proud heritage, abundant resources and skilled and educated people is fully capable of moving toward democracy and living in freedom.[155]

CHAPTER FIVE
THE APPLE SOMETIMES FALLS
CLOSE TO THE TREE

From an Impulsive Reaction
to a Cautious Response

The first Bush administration's decision to go to war ensued within a decision-making structure designed to minimize internal discussion and promote the policy alternative chosen a priori by the president. Bush's choice was not the by-product of a methodical analysis of a range of alternatives. Instead, it was spawned by his instinctive loathing of Saddam Hussein, by his equating of Saddam Hussein to Hitler, and by concluding, based on an examination of the 1938 Munich debacle, that because dictators cannot be appeased his only choice was to act aggressively against the Iraqi leader.

A president can rely on a number of strategies to ensure that he and his advisers analyze and discuss a relatively wide range of options.[1] One of them, "multiple advocacy," requires the president create a structure that enables his advisers to discuss different and, sometimes, opposing perspectives in front of him without fear of repercussion. For this type of exchange to ensue, the president's advisers must have "comparable intelligence, status and clout," and must possess "adequate staff resources."[2] Another approach involves creating a formal policy-development process. Subcommittees prepare carefully crafted option papers, which are then submitted to the president and his immediate advisers for review and decision. And a third method entails the president's bringing together his advisers and their respective immediate subalterns to examine openly and frankly a wide range of alternatives. To enhance the quality of the discussions, the president must, on occasion, leave the gathering area.[3]

At first blush one might be inclined to assume that the first President Bush wanted his senior advisers to feel free to express their opinions. They all knew each other quite well and interacted with one another in an informal and friendly manner. "[W]hen the principals met, Bush liked to keep everyone around the table smiling—jokes, camaraderie, the conviviality of old friends."[4] Interaction among members of the group was "collegial."[5] The reality, however, was markedly more complex.

In order to control the direction of the discussions, he and Scowcroft relied on two interrelated strategies. First, they created a relatively inflexible decision-making hierarchy—one that placed emphasis on each adviser's status and on his field of expertise. As explained earlier, Powell, who had served for a time as national security adviser to President Reagan and thus was well versed in foreign policy matters, was forced by Cheney to recognize and accept that as chairman of the Joint Chiefs of Staff he had to restrict his advice to military issues. "Look," said Cheney to Powell, "you just do military options. Don't be the Secretary of State or the Secretary of Defense or the National Security Adviser. Just do military options."[6]

Second, by August 3, Bush and Scowcroft, with Haass's assistance, had already decided that the United States would have to deploy a very large number of armed personnel in Saudi Arabia. The president concluded that if his administration failed to take a resolute stand against Iraq, the U.S. drive to create a new world order would stall. Washington, moreover, would be signaling to other dictators that they were free to behave badly in the world arena. Though some other members of Bush's decision-making group concurred with the decision, their agreement was not the result of a careful articulation of the problem and a deliberate analysis of a range of options. They did not try to gauge the extent to which Saddam Hussein's decision to invade Kuwait could be linked to one factor instead of another, nor did they attempt to establish how many other actors had resorted to invasion when faced with challenges similar to those encountered by Iraq in 1990. Furthermore, they did not endeavor to predict the various effects the deployment of U.S. forces in Saudi Arabia could spawn.[7] As noted earlier, according to Deputy Secretary of State Eagleburger, the president, by taking a very strong position against Iraq immediately after it invaded Kuwait, "decreased the range of debate on how to approach Iraq, and set the parameters of the agenda on the issue."[8] Wolfowitz provided a related perspective when he expressed concern about the absence of a process that would have required the production of memos discussing a number of alternatives and their possible implications to be submitted for the president's and his closest advisers' consideration.[9]

During the early phase, the first Bush administration examined no more than two options. The first option necessitated only the use of economic sanctions on Iraq; the second alternative entailed both the imposition of economic restrictions and the deployment of U.S. troops on Saudi territory. From a simple comparison of the two choices, it would not be difficult to infer that the second one was substantially more robust than the first. It informed Saddam Hussein not only that the world community (the United Nations) and the United States were determined to inflict heavy economic and financial costs on Iraq if he failed to reverse his action against Kuwait, but also that Washington was prepared to use its military might to prevent him from infringing on Saudi Arabia's sovereignty. In addition, it warned Saddam Hussein that the United States would use its deployed military forces if he did not give Kuwait back its sovereignty. This warning carried on to the second phase, during which time the Bush administration asserted that its choice was between allowing its embargo and containment policy to have its intended effect, or threatening Saddam Hussein with a major attack if he failed to withdraw his forces from Kuwait. The choice, however, was not genuine.

Foreign policy-makers often make decisions based on their interpretations of history. A leader's decision is generally shaped by events that he experienced firsthand or that resonated with him, and by the positive and negative lessons he inferred from them. The systematic foreign policy-maker relies on analogical reasoning, but he does not automatically infer that the analogy or analogies he believes to be relevant will help him address the problem he is striving to resolve.[10] Instead, he attempts to measure the extent to which present and past events correspond in order to ascertain the pertinence of the analogy or analogies. The angry, instinctual foreign policy-maker, on the other hand, compresses reality by matching the present event with a vivid representation of an occurrence he has stored in his memory. His need to analyze whether the present and the old event can be interrelated analogically is weakened substantially if he can interpret both in relatively simple moral terms. Bush behaved as an instinctual foreign policy-maker who chose an analogy early on and stuck to it until the very end.

As someone with extensive foreign policy expertise, Bush, rather than engaging in a careful evaluation of alternatives, tended to trust his "gut." Baker, who had known the president for a long time, confirmed this impression when he remarked, "He made a visceral decision to reverse the decision [Saddam's decision to invade Kuwait] . . ."[11] One gets another glimpse of Bush's propensity to rely on his instincts from his remark to a journalist about a month before he ordered the attack on Iraqi forces. When speculating about whether Saddam Hussein would leave Kuwait, the president responded, "My gut says that he will get out of there."[12]

Bush's primeval response to Saddam Hussein's action in August can be attributed to his belief that the Iraqi leader had duped him.[13] Bush acknowledged as much when he noted that for some time his administration and the previous one "had tried, by selective accommodation, to influence Saddam's behavior. The invasion of Kuwait had betrayed that attempt."[14] Personalizing a challenge was not uncommon for Bush. The secretary of defense revealed this aspect of Bush's character when he warned Admiral Crowe, the former chairman of the Joint Chiefs of Staff, to curb his criticism of the president. Bush, counseled Cheney, "has a long history of vindictive political actions."[15]

Related to Bush's decision to personalize his political dispute with Saddam Hussein was the president's abrupt attempt to depict the Iraqi leader in stark moral tones. For the president, the battle against

Saddam Hussein was reduced, as he acknowledged, "to a very moral case of good versus evil, black versus white." As he told the U.S. Congress, in the Gulf conflict, "Saddam Hussein was the villain, Kuwait the victim." Bush needed to simplify the clash between good and evil in order to justify his resolve and remove all uncertainty. "I've got it boiled down very clearly to good and evil. And it helps if you can be that clear in your mind." The United States had "a clear moral case . . . [n]othing of this moral importance since World War II."[16]

The depiction of Saddam Hussein as evil enabled Bush to connect with his World War II experience, which included his interpretations of Adolf Hitler's behavior, of attempts by the Allied leaders to appease him, and of the consequences of such attempts. Saddam was the new Hitler, hence the new evil. In Bush's own words, the United States was faced with a "Hitler revisited, a totalitarianism and brutality that is naked and unprecedented in modern times."[17] "Appeasement," moreover, "does not work."[18] As proven by the 1938 Munich debacle, the decision by the British, French, and Czech governments to acquiesce to Hitler's demands engendered, ultimately, another worldwide war. Bush sought to give credence to this line of reasoning by referring to Martin Gilbert's *The Second World War: A Complete History*. The lesson that tyrants respond only to exceptional military pressure, explained the president, lay at the core of Gilbert's thesis.[19]

For Bush, sanctions and containment were nothing more than another version of appeasement. Their implementation would shape a new status quo in the Middle East, one that would ultimately degenerate into chaos. As explained by one of his advisers, the president was "deathly afraid of appeasement. His generation had to fight a war over it, and [he] feels that if he blinks today, he will be leaving a real mess for the next generation to clean up. You have an aggressor and if you let him take over Kuwait, he will take over Saudi Arabia and become the paramount power in the Middle East."[20] Baker was not convinced that Bush would give sanctions and containment a chance to force Iraq out of Kuwait. "I thought that the augmentation decision was an extraordinarily significant decision because we could not send that large a force to the Gulf and expect to keep them there, sitting there while we waited months and months for sanctions to work . . ."[21] Cheney concurred with Baker, but in a more definitive way. "[T]he commitment to use force to expel Saddam Hussein from Kuwait was there when the President came down to Camp David that first week into the crisis and said that this aggression will not stand . . . [I]t did not make sense for us to talk about offensive options in August; we didn't have any forces there yet . . ."[22] But it was Haass who ultimately posited the most frank analysis of how he felt about reaching a peaceful resolution. "[P]art of me," he stated, "wanted a peaceful resolution for all the obvious reasons . . . but part of me was extremely worried that if there was a peaceful resolution . . . we would buy ourselves some false time and it would make it much harder to do this sort of thing again . . ."[23]

According to schema theorists, the decision-maker, overwhelmed by sensations and information, seeks to understand the world without using inordinate amounts of energy and time. He compresses reality by matching present experiences with schemas he has stored in his memory from past experiences.[24] In a fashion, the picture depicted by schema theorists helps clarify the president's response to the problem spawned by Iraq's invasion of Kuwait. Bush, as a World War II veteran who had been taught that appeasement does not alter the actions of dictators, considered Munich and its aftermath a pertinent analogy—one that he did not need to revisit to determine its truthfulness and utility. Our present study adds a small, but important, ingredient to that postulate. It suggests that leaders who personalize political disputes may be more predisposed to compress reality, particularly if in the process they can rely on moral language to interweave the problem they are attempting to resolve with lessons they inferred from an earlier one. The import of this added dimension will gain further value in our analysis of the decision by Bush's son to invade Iraq in 2003.

The specters of earlier detrimental events also affected members of the Pentagon. Powell's reluctance to send troops to the Middle East was based on his fear that the military would once again be made the scapegoat of a poorly thought-out policy. "Perhaps I was the ghost of Vietnam, the ghost of Beirut," explained Powell, "and I think as the senior military adviser to the President of the United States and the Secretary of Defense it is my responsibility not only to provide the military options but to help them shape clear political objectives for the military to help achieve."[25] When he realized that Bush was serious about going to war, the chairman of the Chiefs of Staff made sure that if he received the order to attack, his forces would achieve the assigned objective swiftly and at the lowest possible cost. Other Pentagon officials were also determined not to repeat the Vietnam mistakes. The common perception among Powell's colleagues was that the United States's principal error in its war against North Vietnam and the Vietcong had been to assume that if the U.S. military applied force gradually the enemy would be "inspired to sue for peace at an early level of escalation . . ." This gradualist approach, however, gave the other side the time it needed to strengthen its military and solidify its political stand. The lesson: if the United States was to fight a war with a Third World country, it had to use as much firepower as was necessary to quickly destroy the enemy's fighting capability and will. Schwarzkopf verbalized the new doctrine in November 1990 when he stated: "If we go to war, I am going to use every single thing that is available to me to bring as much destruction as I possibly can in the hopes of winning victory as soon as possible."[26] Or, in Powell's words, decisive force announces that if something "is important enough to go to war for, we're going to do it in a way that there's no question what the outcome will be and we're going to do it by putting the force necessary to take the initiative away from your enemy and impose your will upon him. If you're not serious enough to do that, then you ought to think twice about going to war."[27]

Powell and Schwarzkopf had the unwavering support of the president. From the Vietnam War Bush had inferred that if a president decides to go to war, he has to be prepared to let the military make its own choices. As he explained to a group of congressional leaders on November 30: "We don't need another Vietnam War. World unity is there. No hands are going to be tied behind backs. This is not a Vietnam . . . I know whose backside's at stake and rightfully so. It will not be a long, drawn-out mess . . ."[28] Bush kept his word. The president, confirmed Powell, "never told me what to do militarily."[29] Baker concurred by noting that the "President was aware of the experience of Vietnam consistently . . . he knew that the politicians had dictated the war, that it was a limited war, the military had never been able to fight the war they thought they needed to fight to win it and he [the president] was determined to let the military call the shots."[30] The need to avert another Vietnam-type fiasco was also very much in Cheney's mind. In a conversation with the Saudi ambassador, he said: "The military is finished in this society, if we screw this up."[31]

The first Bush administration's decision to stop the war also proceeded along a decision-making path devised to curtail internal debate and endorse the policy favored by the president. Bush's question in February 27, 1991—"Well, if that's the case, we're within the window, why not end it now?"—defined the boundary within which he expected his advisers to assess the news that Iraqi forces had, for all practical purposes, been defeated. But that was not the only limit the president imposed. He also warned his advisers that the administration was "picking up some unfortunate baggage right now, some public baggage." As if to reinforce his apprehension, Bush added: "I'd like you to consider that. I'd like you all to consider that."[32]

Concerns about what to do once the Kuwaiti issue had been resolved did not spring up at the last moment. As preparations for the war ensued, the Bush administration deliberately chose not to draw up a follow-up plan—one designed to overthrow Saddam Hussein's regime. A number of factors contributed to this decision. First, as explained by the U.S. ambassador to Saudi Arabia Chas Freeman the "White House was terrified of leaks about any U.S. plans that might unhinge the huge and unwieldy coalition that George Bush had put together to support the war. Officials were discouraged from writing, talking, or even thinking about what to do" once Kuwait had been liberated.[33] For Bush, Scowcroft, and Baker, who had spent long hours trying to put together a viable alliance, doing anything that could undermine it was unacceptable. They were convinced that any attempt on the part of Washington to go beyond the authorization extended by the UN resolutions would have spawned broad criticism and led some of the United States's Middle Eastern allies to retract their offer to remain members of the coalition forces. This concern retained centrality during the war operations and became one of the main focuses of the Bush administration's discussion as it became evident that Kuwait was about to be freed. Baker made it clear that had the Bush administration proposed at that time to march into Baghdad, it "would have lost [the] coalition. The Arab elements . . . would have left for sure."[34] Powell, forever the reluctant warrior, concurred with Baker. "We had no objective that said go to Baghdad." The United States's Arab friends, Powell added, "were not going to go into Iraq, their soldiers would not step foot in Iraq. They were going into Kuwait to kick the Iraqi army out of Kuwait. That was the resolution passed by the United Nations and that's what the Congressional resolution provided for."[35] Among members of Bush's inner decision-making group, Cheney might have been the most distrustful about the United States's ability to retain the coalition. "I don't think any of our allies would have been with us, maybe Britain, but nobody else."[36] Their apprehension was justified. The leaders of Egypt and Saudi Arabia had already made it quite clear that their troops would not march into Iraq following the liberation of Kuwait.[37]

Retaining the coalition was not the Bush administration's sole concern. Its leading members understood that trying to overthrow and capture Saddam Hussein would have posed an unfathomable military and political challenge. No one described the difficulty of attempting to topple Saddam's regime better than the secretary of defense. Trying to topple the Iraqi regime, explained Cheney,

wasn't anything I was enthusiastic about . . . [T]here was a real danger here that you would get bogged down in a long drawn conflict, that this was a dangerous difficult part of the world . . . [W]e were all worried about the possibility of Iraq coming apart, the Iranians restarting the conflict that they [had] had in the eight-year bloody war with the Iraqis over eastern Iraq . . . Saddam is just one more irritant, but there's a long list of irritants in that part of the world and for us to have done what would have been necessary to get rid of him—certainly a very large force for a long time into Iraq to run him to [the] ground and then you have to worry about what comes after . . . [Y]ou then have to accept responsibility for what happens in Iraq, accept more responsibility for what happens in the region . . . And you are going to take a lot more American casualties if you are going to muck around in Iraq for weeks on end trying to run Saddam Hussein to [the] ground and capture Baghdad and so forth . . . I don't think it would have been worth it.[38]

Bush, Scowcroft, and Baker were equally adamant about not endeavoring to put an end to Saddam Hussein's regime. "Trying to eliminate Saddam, extending the ground war into an occupation of Iraq," argued Bush and Scowcroft, "would have violated our guideline about not changing objectives in midstream, engaging in 'mission creep,' and would have incurred incalculable human and political costs . . . We would have been forced to occupy Baghdad and, in effect, rule Iraq . . . Had we gone the invasion route, the United States could conceivably [remain an occupying power for an extended period] in a bitterly hostile land."[39] Baker, as the attentive diplomat, was determined not to disregard the Saudis' stipulation for backing the invasion. The Saudis "wanted us to leave as promptly as possible—get our forces out of there at the end of the war—when there was a question of whether we should occupy some of southern Iraq."[40]

The first Bush administration's apprehension about the problems it would encounter if it tried to topple Saddam's regime was compounded by the worry that finding and capturing the Iraqi leader would be a nearly insurmountable military task. Its anxiety was the result of an earlier experience. In December 1989, less than a year after becoming president, Bush ordered the invasion of Panama. His objective was to topple and capture its strongman, Manuel Noriega. Trying to find Noriega proved to be a much more difficult mission than initially expected. The effect of this experience on Bush and Scowcroft was considerable. When "we went into Panama," explained Scowcroft, "we [could not] find Noriega even though we knew Panama like the back of our hands and we knew every place that he usually stayed. We had no way of finding Saddam in Iraq." He and Bush reaffirmed their concern when they wrote: "Apprehending him

[Saddam} was probably impossible. We had been unable to find Noriega in Panama, which we knew intimately."[41]

Severe nervousness prompted by the criticism the United States was enduring for its actions, along with a considerable measure of wishful thinking, were the last two factors that helped convince Bush and his chief advisers that they needed to bring the war to an end rapidly. By February 27 it had become evident amongst all observers not just that Iraq lacked the means to fend off the coalition forces, but also that as its forces retreated they were absorbing a very large number of casualties. In what came to be known as the "highway to hell," allied assault aircrafts launched, in the words of Colin Smith of the *London Observer*, "one of the most terrible harassments of a retreating army . . . in the history of warfare."[42] The carnage troubled the Bush administration. "[T]o continue the war," explained Scowcroft, "would have been an unnecessary slaughter of people who at that point could not defend themselves." The continuation of the war, moreover, was beginning to raise moral questions and making bad copy in newspapers and television screens, with some describing the attacks as "turkey shoots."[43] The Bush administration, added Scowcroft, could not afford to "look like butchers who were bent on revenge by slaughtering people."[44] Baker viewed the effect of the bloodshed somewhat differently. "Iraq was out of Kuwait. The Iraqis were taking rather massive casualties on the Highway of Death." To keep attacking would have been "sort of un-American."[45] Haass had a similar explanation of his superiors' rationale. In his view, the Bush administration did not want to be accused of engaging in unsportsmanlike behavior—"of piling on once the whistle had blown."[46]

Lastly, the Bush administration could not escape its practice of engaging in wishful thinking. As explained earlier, in late July 1990, though fully aware that Saddam Hussein had deployed some 100,000 Iraqi troops close to the Kuwaiti border, the Bush administration's senior members refused to consider the possibility that the Iraqi leader intended to invade Kuwait. Some seven months later, the president and many of his senior advisers became convinced that the war and its dreadful consequences would compel the Iraqi military to oust

Saddam Hussein. As explained by Scowcroft, "We had high expectations that the military suffering the kind of defeat they had would turn on Saddam. They didn't . . . [W]e underestimated his ability at survival."[47] Haass agreed with his boss's assessment. The common belief, noted Haass, was that "Saddam would be overthrown by his own people, probably from the military, who would have essentially been fed up with the fact that this character had twice marched them off into disaster within a decade. And our view was that whilst we couldn't guarantee, it was the most likely course of action. Events were simply left to themselves."[48] Cheney, though more guarded with his prediction, concurred. There was the "belief on the part of many of the experts and others in the region that if you administer a decisive defeat to his [Saddam Hussein's] military forces that he will not be able to survive politically."[49] For a brief while, the end of the war seemed to have done little to induce the Bush administration to alter its thinking. As Washington and the rest of the world watched Iraq being engulfed by internal violence, Bush continued to believe that the Iraqi leader would not be able to "survive." "[P]eople," claimed the president, "are fed up with him. They see him for the brutal dictator he is."[50]

The last assessments were not built on a solid foundation. As explained by a veteran of CIA operations in Iraq, "All the analysts in State, CIA, DIA, NSA were in agreement with the verdict that Saddam was going to fall. There wasn't a single dissenting voice. The only trouble was, they had no hard data at all. Their whole way of thinking really was conditioned on a Western way of looking at things. A leader such as Saddam who had been defeated and humiliated would have to leave office. Just that. Plus, none of these analysts had ever set foot in Iraq. Not one."[51]

In short, when the time came to decide whether to prolong the war or bring it to a close, Bush had no choice but to put aside his personal loathing of the Iraqi leader. In his estimation, the costs of marching into Baghdad would have outweighed the benefits principally because he assumed that the United States's chances of toppling Saddam Hussein's regime, capturing him, and putting in place a new, stable, pro-U.S. government were diminutive. His advisers agreed. Even before circumstances compelled them to decide whether to invade Iraq for the purpose of overthrowing its regime and capturing its leader, they had concluded that any attempt on the part of the United States to occupy Iraq would spawn a highly critical and divisive response from its main allies in the Middle East.[52] They deemed such an outcome unacceptable. Though they did not regard guarding the coalition as important as forcing Iraq's forces out of Kuwait, they ranked it high. Their estimation that the coalition would collapse were the United States to invade Iraq was not the result of a misconception. The leaders of Egypt and Saudi Arabia made it abundantly clear that they would not support an allied invasion of Iraq and that they expected the United States to leave the region shortly after the Iraqi forces had been expelled from Kuwait.

Of nearly equal significance was their calculation that occupying Iraq would generate some grave long-term human and political costs. They predicted that such an act would tear Iraq apart, entice Iran to renew the 1980s conflict, and obligate the United States to accept greater responsibility for Iraq and the region's future. Though they would have liked to see Saddam Hussein vanish from the Middle Eastern political environment, they viewed him as little more than another irritant, one that the United States could contain. The benefits of getting rid of Saddam Hussein, they estimated, would not offset the costs of getting bogged down in a prolonged conflict.

With the help of hindsight, it is sensible to speculate whether the Bush administration would have still decided not to occupy Iraq if its senior members, the U.S. intelligence community, and Washington's Middle Eastern friends had predicted that Saddam Hussein's military would not remove him from power. Bearing in mind the weight Bush and his inner decision-making circle placed on protecting the integrity of the coalition and averting a protracted and costly involvement, it seems realistic to surmise that the United States would have not invaded Iraq. As Cheney noted, Saddam Hussein was just another irritant, and the United States had no obligation to get rid of every one of them so long as they could be contained.

Inadequate Information, Wishful Thinking, and Foreign Policy-Making

Defining an international problem is not particularly cumbersome if the definers have on hand substantial amounts of reliable information. Foreign policy-makers, however, do not always have the means to gauge the quality of the information they possess or know whether they have enough information to define a problem correctly. In chapter four we sought to demonstrate that throughout 2002 and the early part of 2003, the senior members in the second Bush administration knew, despite some of their public pronouncements, that they did not have "irrefutable evidence" to prove that the regime of Saddam Hussein was rebuilding its nuclear weapons program or that it had links to al Qaeda and had helped orchestrate the September 11, 2001 attacks on the United States. What is more, they had ample historical evidence that cast considerable doubt on the U.S. ability to transform Iraq into a stable democratic state. Because the first misstep in a rational process can materialize during the definition of a problem, we will explain why many of the leading members of the second Bush administration decided Iraq posed a major and direct threat to the United States, and became convinced that building a stable democracy in Iraq would not be a laborious and costly endeavor.

During the 1990s and the early years of the new millennium, U.S. antagonism toward Iraq went through phases—it boiled during the first Bush administration, but then simmered while Clinton occupied the White House. During Clinton's presidency, neither he nor any of his senior advisers seriously considered launching an invasion to topple Saddam Hussein's regime. Washington began to look at Iraq through a somewhat different lens with the arrival of the new administration. In early January 2001, Vice-President-elect Cheney asked the retiring secretary of defense William Cohen for a briefing, at which time they would hold a serious "discussion about Iraq and different options." The briefing, which took place on January 10, did not amount to much. The generals who briefed the incoming president and his entourage delineated the various operations the Pentagon had carried out against Saddam Hussein, but did not discuss the possibility of launching a major ground operation. The common sentiment at the Pentagon was that Saddam Hussein had been contained and isolated, and that any attempt to initiate strong action against the Iraqi regime would immediately engender strong opposition in the region and throughout the world. At a second national security briefing a few days later, this one given by the CIA, Bush and his advisers heard little about Iraq.[53]

For the next several months, the new principals and their deputies discussed Iraq and how to undermine its regime. On August 1, the Deputies Committee, headed by Hadley, submitted to the principals a document titled *A Liberation Strategy*. The paper discussed ways in which the United States, through a phase strategy, could help destabilize the Iraqi regime. Though the deputies considered the circumstances under which the United States might use its military power directly, they never presented them in the document.[54] All in all, despite the fact that some of the leading civilian officials at the Pentagon, with Wolfowitz as the chief advocate, had believed for some time that the United States should get rid of Saddam Hussein and that such an endeavor would not be particularly difficult, the idea was never formally presented to Bush and his most senior advisers prior to September 11. This compels us, therefore, to try to decipher what swayed them to elevate Iraq to the top of their foreign policy agenda after September 11.

As explained in the earlier case, foreign policy-makers rely on history to define problems. Using incomplete information, they count on contextual factors associated with critical past occurrences to impose interpretations on new issues. The use of an analogy suggests disinterest on the part of a foreign policy-maker to ascertain the extent to which aspects of a present event may differ from a past one.[55] Often, the end-result of this process is the introduction of biases and distortion into the analysis of a set of political events.[56]

Analogies influenced the Bush administration's decision-making process in decisive, but different, ways. For Wolfowitz, a former scholar, Hitler's behavior was a reliable analogy. During Hitler's rearmament of Germany, argued the deputy secretary of defense, "the world's hollow warnings formed weak defenses." During Hitler's annexation of Austria, "the world sat by." The "world sat still" when Hitler's forces marched into Czechoslovakia prior to the war. And when Britain and France warned Hitler to leave Poland alone, he disregarded their warning.[57] Saddam Hussein's behavior and the manner in which much of the world had been responding to it, concluded Wolfowitz, were markedly similar to the interaction between Hitler and the international community in the 1930s. Others placed most of the emphasis on Saddam Hussein's earlier behavior and assumed that it would be a good prognosticator of what he was doing or intended to do. His invasion of Kuwait had gone contrary to the initial expectations of the first Bush administration. From then on, some of its senior members, Cheney among them, viewed the Iraqi leader as evil, power-hungry, and menacing. They shared the sentiment expressed by the director of Gulf affairs in Clinton's NSC, Kenneth Pollack, that Saddam Hussein was "one of the most reckless, aggressive, violence-prone, risk-tolerant, and damage-tolerant leaders of modern history."[58] And, as explained by Rice, because of Saddam Hussein's earlier actions, "the president of the United States could not afford to trust Saddam's motives or give him the benefit of the doubt."[59] In their view, although they did not have firm new information indicating Saddam Hussein's regime was rebuilding its nuclear program and working with al Qaeda insurgents, what they had, in the words of Bush's CIA director, was "consistent with the pattern of deception and denial exhibited by Saddam Hussein over the past 12 years."[60] The fact that between 1991 and 1995 the CIA had concluded that Iraq had developed many more weapons than initially estimated, and that had the first Bush administration not intervened to free Kuwait in 1991 Iraq might have produced a usable nuclear weapon by December 1992, was enough to generate reasonable fears.[61] Given the history of Iraq's weapons programs, explained Kerr, it "would have been very hard for any group of analysts, looking at the situation between 1991 through 1995, to conclude that the WMD were not under way." Once the inspectors left, he added, "it was also hard to prove they weren't under way."[62] Or, as Rumsfeld and Wolfowitz liked to contend, "the lack of evidence did not mean something did not exist."[63]

The president approached the past in his own unique way. Prior to September 11, no single earlier event seemed to affect how he viewed Iraq. He knew that his father had once been the target of an assassination attempt ordered by Saddam Hussein. He was aware also that Cheney, Wolfowitz, and Feith had been discussing the idea of the United States's altering the status quo in Iraq, and had been contending that the task would not be formidable. Initially Bush listened, and said little. In a discussion with Powell, who believed that some of the president's advisers' ideas about Iraq were unsound, the president stated: "[I]t is a good contingency plan and I know what they are doing and I'm in no hurry to go look for trouble."[64] After September 11, the president did not give in right away to those who argued that the United States should move aggressively against Iraq. Determined to signal the world that the United States was not "impotent," he ordered the Pentagon to design immediately a response against the state that housed Osama bin Laden and al Qaeda. Bush believed that any attempt on the part of his administration to implement, concurrently, aggressive responses against Afghanistan and Iraq would be exceedingly complex, and that such a dual effort would undermine the United States's ability to respond rapidly against those who were known to have originated the attacks. "My theory," he stated, "is you've got to do something and do it well ... if we could prove that we could be successful in [the Afghanistan] theater, then the rest of the task would be easier. If we tried to do too many things—two things, for example, or three things—militarily, then ... the lack of focus would have been a huge risk."[65] He also emphasized that he would not let the previous experience by some of his advisers "in this theater [Iraq] dictate a rational course of action."[66] Still, he did not dismiss the notion of focusing on Iraq at a later time. As he said to Rice: "We won't do Iraq now, we are putting Iraq off. But eventually we will have to return to that question."[67] And he did.

Ten days after he had been informed that the coalition forces in Afghanistan would be victorious, he ordered Rumsfeld to start looking into what it would take to depose the Iraqi leader. September 11 altered his mindset and the opportunity on the part of some of his principal foreign policy-advisers to assert that Iraq should be the United States's next target. As underscored by a senior administrator, without September 11, those who for quite some time had favored removing Saddam Hussein from power "never would have been able to put Iraq at the top of our agenda. It was only then that this president was willing to worry about the unthinkable— that the next attack could be with weapons of mass destruction supplied by Saddam Hussein."[68] Bush acknowledged as much when he stated that before September 11 he had largely ignored terrorism. "I didn't feel that sense of urgency. My blood was not nearly boiling."[69] September 11 became, as he noted in his diary, the "Pearl Harbor of the twenty-first century."[70] After that day, Saddam Hussein's "terrible features became much more threatening. He had used weapons of mass destruction in the past. He has created incredible instability in the region."[71] Rice echoed the president's sentiment when she stated that September 11 "was one of the great earthquakes that clarify and sharpen. Events are in much sharper relief."[72] But it was Rumsfeld who best summarized the effect of September 11 on the Bush administration's senior members. We, stated Rumsfeld, "did not act in Iraq because we had discovered dramatic new evidence of Iraq's pursuit of weapons of mass destruction. We acted because we saw the existing evidence in a new light, through the prism of our experience on September 11."[73]

These answers, however, still fail to explain why Iraq became a target of the United States's wrath and not North Korea or Iran. After all, the actions of the other two adversaries were also thought to be highly problematic. The analysis of a president's personal idiosyncrasies and their effects on his decisions is a subject that often generates controversy among political scientists. Given that there is so much disagreement about how personality affects a leader's political behavior, their skepticism is justified. Still, a few of the ideas posited by certain scholars are worth bearing in mind when analyzing Bush's decision to focus on Iraq after he learned that the coalition forces had nearly achieved their principal objectives in Afghanistan.

James Barber has argued that some presidents are stimulated by social needs, some by cognition, some by emotional needs, and still others by a sense of duty.[74] Though it is difficult to state with great confidence that Bush was motivated by any one of the conditions suggested by Barber, it is reasonable to contend, as the president himself acknowledged, that the idea of promoting liberty inspired him.[75] During the period he contemplated the idea of going to war against Iraq, Bush did not seem terribly concerned about the way history would eventually judge him.[76] As he once noted, sardonically: "We won't know. We will all be dead."[77] Nonetheless, he believed, as mentioned before, that he was president "for a reason"—to propagate worldwide the vision of the United States as "liberator." Moreover, he viewed the September 11 attacks as justification for promoting what in his mind were universal ideals. I am convinced, he observed, that "[t]his [September 11] is a great opportunity."[78] The "United States is the beacon for freedom in the world [and it has] a responsibility to promote freedom that is as solemn as the responsibility is to protecting the American people, because the two go hand-in-hand."[79] Did he think that a deity had anointed him to carry out such mission? No and yes. "I am surely not going to justify the war based on God . . . Nevertheless, in my case, I pray to be as good a messenger of his will as possible."[80] God might not have ordered Bush to promote freedom worldwide, but the president seemed to assume that he had a good idea what God's will was.

As a politician who lacked international experience and "curiosity about complex issues," whose "leadership style bordered on the hurried," and who demanded immediate action and solutions, Bush viewed Iraq as the instrument that would enable him and the United States to further promote his goals rapidly and at a relatively low cost.[81] He understood that though the international hazards generated by Iran and North Korea were greater than the threat posed by Iraq, any attempt on the part of the United States to intimidate

Tehran or Pyongyang with war would have engendered excessive risks. The tasks of defeating Saddam Hussein and transforming Iraq into a stable democracy, he assumed, would be markedly less daunting. These two assumptions did not exist independently. To capture their interrelationship, it is imperative to focus on the second assumption and on how the Bush administration went about planning the democratization of Iraq.

A good starting point is December 28, 2001 when General Franks presented the initial war plan to the president in Crawford, Texas. The presentation was transmitted via secure video links to Powell, Rice, and Tenet in Washington; Rumsfeld in Taos, New Mexico; and Cheney in Wyoming. When asked by Bush whether the plan was "good enough to win," the general responded that it was, but added that it needed some fine-tuning.[82] Neither the president nor any of his advisers inquired what the United States would have to do in order to stabilize the country, start the reconstruction process, and establish a new democratic government following the demise of the Saddam Hussein regime. The posing of such questions at that stage were essential mainly because had Franks prepared and presented a comprehensive analysis that concluded the postwar reconstruction period would be perilous, costly, and lengthy, those listening to his presentation would have been forced to view the decision to go to war through a different prism.

Despite the fact that not one of the top foreign policy-makers sought to inquire what it would take to transform Iraq into a relatively secure democracy, the issue soon attracted the interest of the Department of State. In April 2002, it put together a group of some 200 Iraqi lawyers, engineers, business people, and other experts to examine the problems the United States and its allies would have to address during the post–Saddam Hussein era.[83] As explained by Zalmay Khalilzad, a special assistant to the president and the senior director of Near East, South West Asian, and North African Affairs, *The Future of Iraq Project* was established to address three challenges: (i) how to reconstruct Iraq's political system, (ii) how to rebuild Iraq's economy, and (iii) how to ensure that Iraq would be secure and that its people would be ruled by laws and not by force.[84] The following

month, Franks and the Pentagon's Joint Staff began to design a plan
to stabilize Iraq after the toppling of the Saddam Hussein regime.[85]
Franks and his colleagues, however, did not intend to address the
types of measures the United States would have to carry out in order
to set up a democratic regime in Iraq.

By the end of 2002, differences about what plan the United States
should adopt had surfaced. According to the director of planning at
the Department of State, disagreements revolved around questions
such as: "What number of American troops [should the United
States deploy]? How much to bring in others [allies]? What should
be the role of the United Nations [in the reconstruction]? What
should be the pace of Iraqi-zation?" Answers varied, depending on
the participants' expectations with regard to: "What would be the
Iraqi reaction? How difficult would this [the reconstruction] likely
be? What kind of resistance could we [the United States] expect?"[86]
Such divergences, moreover, were the result of, and elicited, substantial
bureaucratic turf infighting. Richard Perle, who had served as chairman of the Defense Policy Board and was a close political ally of
Cheney, Rumsfeld, and Wolfowitz, claimed that the CIA and the
Department of State resisted postwar planning. Kanan Makiya, who
had close ties to the Pentagon and was an adviser to the Iraqi
National Congress, was also highly critical of the role played by the
Department of State, particularly regarding its unwillingness to
address political problems during the postwar period. Laith Kubba,
on the other hand, as president of Iraq National Group, was critical
of Cheney, Perle, and Wolfowitz. He alleged that the three had had
"an agenda to bring [down] Saddam Hussein by war" and wanted to
"dominate the whole process from A to Z, and they wanted all other
players, Iraqi, Americans, and others, more or less to follow their
rules . . ."[87]

In early January 2003, Douglas Feith, the undersecretary for
policy at the Pentagon, suggested to Hadley the setting up of an inter-
agency planning cell at the Department of Defense. Its task would be
to implement the stabilization policy. The cell, according to Feith,
would receive policy guidance from the deputies committee and the

principals, but would assume responsibility for designing and carrying out the plan. Powell did not object. With very little discussion, the president signed National Security Presidential Directive #24. The classified document authorized the Department of Defense to set up the Office of Reconstruction and Humanitarian Assistance (ORHA), with the tasks of both planning and implementing the plans. Rumsfeld chose an old acquaintance, retired Army Lieutenant General Jay M. Garner, to lead ORHA. The Department of State, in the meantime, was ordered to send over the "Future of Iraq" study along with the names of 75 Arab experts. Thomas Warrick and Meghan Sullivan were assigned to head the Department of State team. Powell soon learned that Rumsfeld had ordered the leaders of the team to leave the Pentagon, and questioned the action. Postwar planning, argued Rumsfeld, could not include people who were not fully supportive of the policy Bush was striving to implement. Cheney was the force behind this demand. He believed that the United States had "an obligation to stand up for democracy. We can't get some former [Iraqi] general and put him in charge and say, Okay, now you're the dictator in Iraq. We've got to fundamentally change the place. And we've got to give the Iraqi people a chance at those fundamental values we believe in."[88]

On March 4, Feith briefed the president and the NSC on the Department of Defense postwar goals. The objectives identified under the heading of *U.S. and Coalition Objectives* were:

1. Maintaining Iraq's territorial integrity and improving substantially the quality of life in Iraq.
2. Helping create democratic institutions throughout Iraq so that the world would see that it is moving toward democracy. Promoting it as a model for the region.
3. Upholding freedom of action for the U.S. and coalition forces so that they can continue to carry out the global war on terrorism and capture and destroy WMD.
4. Obtaining international participation in the reconstruction endeavor.

5. Gaining the support of the Iraqi people.
6. Getting the political support of the international community, including the regional states, if at all possible through a UN Security Council Resolution.
7. Placing Iraqis in positions of physical authority as soon as possible.
8. Accomplishing all of the above rapidly.[89]

Four aspects of the Pentagon's plan were unique. First, in their new design the planners paid little attention to the information gathered by the Department of State and incorporated few of its recommendations. As noted by a senior Pentagon official, "it was mostly ignored."[90] More to the point, Rumsfeld instructed Garner, the recently appointed "American proconsul," not to use the work.[91] Second, though the Department of Defense identified its objectives for the postwar period, it did not set up a clearly delineated plan that explained how they would be fulfilled. As explained by Major Isaiah Wilson III, there "was no adequate operational plan for stability operations and support operations."[92] Third, the plan was designed almost at the last hour. And fourth, there was substantial concern, inside and outside the Bush administration, that the United States would not have sufficient forces to be effective during the reconstruction phase and that its expectations about how long it would take to pacify the country were unrealistic.

Points two, three, and four require additional discussion. Constructing a democracy in a state that never had one requires careful planning. The maximum time the Bush administration gave itself to design a postwar plan was 12 months. However, given that the project designed by the Department of State was largely ignored, it is reasonable to conclude that the Department of Defense gave itself only four months to develop a reconstruction plan. This figure compares poorly with the three years spent by the Roosevelt administration preparing for the postwar reconstruction of Germany. In 1942, the Army War College set up a School of Military Government at the University of Virginia to think about the postwar reconstruction of its adversary. The outcome of this initiative was *Operation ECLIPSE*, and from its implementation the designers and others concluded that "a long detailed planning process far in advance of the start of occupation" was imperative.[93]

Point four is partly related to the earlier two. In a confidential briefing prepared for Rice and Hadley, titled "Force Security in Seven Recent Stability Operations," their military aides in the NSC argued that maintaining security after defeating the enemy was "determined by an entirely different set of calculations, including the population, the scope of the terrain and the necessary tasks." It also pointed out that more "forces generally are required to control countries with large urban populations." If the Bush administration used Kosovo as its benchmark, it would need 480,000; if it used Bosnia, it would need 364,000; but if it used Afghanistan, then it would need only 13,900. Both the White House and the Department of Defense rejected the Balkans as a model to be emulated. In a speech titled "Beyond Nation Building," delivered in New York on February 14, 2003, Rumsfeld stated that the large number of troops in the Balkans had helped create a "culture of dependence," which discouraged local inhabitants from taking responsibilities for themselves. For Rumsfeld, Afghanistan was the better model. The secretary of defense's commitment to the alternative model was confirmed by Secretary of the Army Thomas E. White, who noted: "Our working budgetary assumption was that 90 days after completion of the operation, we would withdraw the first 50,000 and then every 30 days we'd take out another 50,000 until everybody was back. The view was that whatever was left in Iraq would be *de minimis*."[94] Or, in the words of Lieutenant Colonel Michael Hamm, a spokesman for Feith, the "plan is to get it done as quickly as possible and get out."[95]

Plans are built on a mixture of knowledge, assumptions, and convictions. Based on past experiences, the Bush administration could have inferred that stabilizing Iraq and creating a democratic regime in Iraq would be an unwieldy job, and that to succeed it would have to deploy a large number of forces. Bush had been warned by one of his senior advisers that if he declared war on Iraq and defeated Saddam Hussein, the stabilization and reconstruction processes would be arduous and lengthy. Powell had told him so during one of their private meetings, and the president understood that the secretary of state was alerting him "that if in fact Saddam is toppled by military [invasion], we better have a strong understanding about what it's going to take to rebuild Iraq."[96] More importantly, in January 2003, Bush received two reports prepared by the National Intelligence Council, an independent group that advises the director of the CIA. In one of the assessments, the National Intelligence Council—the same council that argued that, if desperate, Saddam Hussein might decide to aid a terrorist organization such as al Qaeda—predicted that a U.S.-led invasion "of Iraq would increase support for political Islam and would result in a deeply divided Iraqi society prone to violent internal conflict." Another important conclusion it arrived at was that "rogue elements from Saddam Hussein's government could work with existing terrorist groups or act independently to wage guerrilla warfare . . . [and that] a war would increase sympathy across the Islamic world for some terrorist objectives . . ."[97]

The earlier mentioned information, however, was offset by a number of assumptions, inferences, and opinions. As explained by Rice, the first assumption was that the United States "would defeat the army, but the institutions would hold, everything from ministries to police forces." The Bush administration would "bring in new leadership" but keep "the body in place."[98] Additionally, it assumed that if the United States proved to be successful during its struggle against Saddam Hussein, the event would rapidly spawn additional positive results, both outside and inside Iraq. Despite the fact that some of the world's major powers had opposed the war, the vice president and the president were convinced that as soon as the United States defeated Iraq, those who had questioned his policy would put their objections aside and provide military support.[99] This type of thinking was new for the vice president.

As explained earlier, in 1991, in response to whether the United States should continue the war against Iraq after expelling Saddam

Hussein's forces from Kuwait, Cheney explained why it should not. "Once you've got Baghdad," noted the then secretary of defense, "it's not clear what you do with it. It's not clear what kind of government you would put in place of the one that's currently there now. Is it going to be a [Shiite] regime, or Sunni regime or a Kurdish regime? Or one that tilts towards the Baathists, or one that tilts towards the Islamic fundamentalists? How much credibility is that government going to have if it's set up by the United States military when it's there? How long does the United States military have to stay to protect the people that sign on for that government, and what happens to it when it leaves?" However, by August 2002, Cheney, as vice president, had changed his mind. Using Professor Fouad Ajami as one of his sources, Cheney told a large group of veterans of foreign wars that after "liberation the streets of Basra and Baghdad are 'sure to erupt in joy in the same way the throngs in Kabul greeted the Americans.' "[100]

Bush concurred. He believed that "confident action that will yield positive results, provides kind of a slipstream into which reluctant nations and leaders can get behind and show themselves that . . . something positive has happened toward peace."[101] Bush was also certain that success would kindle similar responses from the Iraqis. "[F]reedom," he claimed, "is something people long for. And . . . if given a chance, the Iraqis over time would seize the moment."[102] Bush deemed his confidence in the Iraqis justified. During a private meeting at the White House with three Iraqi dissidents in January 2003, one of them said: "People will greet troops with flowers." "How do you know?" asked Bush. The information, they responded, is coming from inside Iraq, from the people. By the end of the meeting Bush was so pleased with what he had been told that he said: "Maybe one year from now we will be toasting victory and talking about the transition to freedom."[103] He carried the excitement to his May 6, 2003, speech at the American Enterprise Institute. In Germany and Japan, he explained, the United States left behind "an atmoshphere of safety in which responsible, reform-minded local builders could build lasting institutions of freedom."[104] The same experience would be replicated in Iraq.

Top civilian officials at the Pentagon agreed with their president. In the words of Lieutenant Colonel Joseph Apodaca, a U.S. Marine intelligence officer, the Pentagon designed its plan based on the assumption that "when people realized that he [Saddam Hussein] was gone, that would get the population on our side and facilitate the transition to reconstruction."[105] Much of the transition, moreover, would be handled by expatriates favored by the Pentagon, such as Ahmed Chalabi, who would rapidly transform Iraq into a democratic state.[106] Rumsfeld, who believed that were the United States to send a large military contingency it would create a detrimental "culture of dependence"—an ethos that would discourage Iraqis from taking responsibility for their future—did nothing to discourage such expectations.[107] In short, Bush contemplated three attractive prospects: toppling Saddam Hussein without imposing intolerable costs on the United States, stimulating the birth of democracy in Iraq, and using the transformation as the model to spawn a democratic domino effect throughout the region. These were alluring incentives to a president who by the end of 2001 viewed himself as the leader of the global liberation movement, thus disregarding the warning by the highly respected British military historian Liddell Hart, who noted that leaders must "[a]void self-righteousness like the devil" because "nothing is so self-blinding."[108]

In an ideal world, evaluating alternatives and making a final choice would be tasks independent of the identification and definition of a problem. In the real world, they are often tightly interlinked. The second Bush administration made a decision to elevate Iraq to the top of its agenda, along with a claim that Saddam Hussein was committed to establishing an association with al Qaeda members and that his past behavior confirmed that he was too irresponsible, unyielding, and belligerent to be permitted to have WMD. This decision and claim affected the number and types of alternatives the administration assessed and the policy it selected.[109]

When Bush ordered Rumsfeld to begin assessing what it would take to depose Saddam Hussein, he did not ask his secretary of defense what he thought about the U.S. policy of containment or whether deterrence would be a viable alternative. By not posing either question, the president was conveying two distinct ideas. First, he was indicating that he was prepared to renounce the continuing implementation of containment and that he believed deterrence would not have the intended effect on the Iraqi leader. "The options in Iraq," argued the president, "were relatively limited when you are playing the containment game."[110] And, as his September 2002 *National Security Strategy of the United States of America* document made clear: Deterrence "based only upon the threat of retaliation is less likely to work against leaders of rogue states more willing to take risks, gambling with the lives of their people, and the wealth of their nations . . ." Second, if containment and deterrence were unlikely to be effective, then so would a much less forceful alternative such as diplomacy.

The nearly outright exclusion of three alternatives left the Bush administration with few choices. In early January 2002, Tenet went to the White House to inform the president that a covert operation would not bring Saddam Hussein down. Unhappy with the news, the president ordered Tenet to design plans to support the U.S. military in an operation to overthrow the Iraqi regime. A little over a month later, Bush signed a secret intelligence order directing the CIA to start covert action to support a military operation to overthrow Saddam Hussein with a budget of $200 million. The authorization came just a few days after Franks had presented to the president and NSC members an improved Generated Start Plan for war against Iraq.[111] Never during this period did Bush and his senior advisers hold a meeting designed to compare with other alternatives the benefits and costs of going to war against Iraq and trying to replace it with a stable democracy.

Deep reluctance on the part of some of the leading members within the Bush administration to consider other options eroded briefly when the president acquiesced to Powell's private request to give diplomacy a chance. On August 5, after attending a meeting in which Franks presented the latest revision of his military plan, Powell, concerned by the failure on Bush's part to discuss with his senior advisers whether going to war was the best course of action, asked to meet with him in private.[112] During the meeting Powell warned the president about the pitfalls of war and recommended that the United States try to internationalize the problem through the UN.[113] On September 7, 2002, members of the NSC met to decide what approach to take vis-à-vis the United Nations. To protect the credibility of the United States, argued Powell, it was important to go to the UN and propose resolutions that would facilitate the restart of inspections. Cheney disagreed. The inspectors, proposed the vice president, would be lawyers and experts from around the world, not Americans; consequently, they would be less skeptical of Saddam Hussein. Moreover, they would be inclined to accept the Iraqis' version about their WMD programs. The end result, proposed the vice president, would be inconclusive reports. Aware that for domestic and international political reasons he could not sidestep the UN issue, Bush agreed to involve the organization. Five days later, the president went to the UN and stated what Powell had wanted: "We will work with the UN Security Council for the necessary resolutions."[114]

Bush's declaration lacked commitment. The only thing that would have persuaded Bush that war was not a justifiable choice would have been the relinquishing of power by Saddam Hussein and his top leaders, and the replacing of his regime by a pro-U.S. government. Many of his advisers knew that the president would most likely go to war long before he formally announced his decision. By Christmas 2001, Libby, Cheney's chief of staff and national security adviser, had concluded, after learning that the president had ordered Rumsfeld to start looking into ways to topple Saddam Hussein, that Bush "was well on the road to deposing" the Iraqi leader.[115] On March 21, 2002, Franks warned some of his top commanders to take seriously the secretary of defense's order to develop a viable war plan. "You know," said the general, "if you guys think this is not going to happen, you're wrong. You need to get off your ass."[116] By July 2002, Haass had deduced that the United States "had lit a fuse" and would in all probability go to war.[117] During the same month, members of Tony Blairs's cabinet learned from the director of MI6, who had just returned from a visit to Washington, that military "action was now seen as inevitable." In his report, the director added that the president "wanted to remove Saddam through military action" and would use as his justification the "conjunction of terrorism and WMD."[118] And by early September, even the White House legislative affairs director Nick Calio, though not privy to the discussions that ensued amongst the principals, had come to realize that the "question on Iraq was not if but when there would be war."[119]

New doubts about the merits of going to war could have arisen in mid-October, when the secretary of defense sent the president a memo with a long list of things that could go wrong. The memo, however, was not sent with the intent of suggesting that Bush and his senior advisers should revisit the idea of going to war and compare the option with other alternatives. First, as Rumsfeld conceded, he sent the memo to prepare the president "for what could go wrong, to prepare so things would go right." Second, at the end of the memo Rumsfeld wrote: "Note: It is possible, of course, to prepare a similar illustrative list of all the potential problems that need to be considered if there is no regime change in Iraq." The note is telling in two distinct ways. First, it admitted that the memo was designed to point out potential problems rather than to provide the president the opportunity to conduct a systematic comparison of options. Second, it was written based on the assumption that it was imperative to bring about regime change in Iraq, and that it could happen only if the United States went to war.[120]

Additional concerns about resorting to war could have been voiced during the months preceding the final decision. By December, however, Bush and some of his leading advisers had decided that the United States would go to war, regardless of what new intelligence might reveal. The month before, the UN Security Council had approved Resolution 1441. It called for the restart of weapons inspections on the ground in Iraq and for a full weapons declaration by the regime. For some at the White House, the resolution placed the Iraqi leader in a no-win situation. "If Saddam Hussein indicated that he has weapons of mass destruction and that he is violating United Nations resolution," noted the White House's press secretary, "then we will know that Saddam Hussein again deceived the world. If he declared that he had none, then we will know that Saddam Hussein is once again misleading the world."[121] The Bush administration, thus, posited the justifications it would need to launch a major military operation against Iraq regardless of how Saddam Hussein responded.

The Bush administration also distrusted the UN weapons inspectors. When Rice informed Bush in late December 2002 that the weapons inspectors had yet to uncover anything of great significance in Iraq, the president responded angrily: "I am not sure this is going to work." He then asked Rice, for the first time: "Should we do this [go to war]?" Her response was an emphatic "Yes." A few days after the start of the new year, the president once again voiced his concern to the national security adviser about the weapons inspectors' role. "The United States," he said, "can't stay in this position while Saddam plays games with the inspectors . . . He's getting more confident, not less. He can manipulate the international system again. We are not winning. Time is not on our side. Probably going to have to, we're going to have to go to war." When the director of IAEA announced in late January 2003 that the weapons inspectors had not found evidence to substantiate the claim that Iraq had restarted its nuclear program and that in the next few months they would be able to prove it did not have one, the president dismissed the conclusion. His frustration was compounded by China's, Russia's and France's contention that the inspections were useful and that the UN Security Council should not alter its course unless the inspectors acknowledged they were no longer able to do their job in Iraq. On March 7, the IAEA forwarded a more definitive assessment: "[W]e have to date found no evidence or plausible indication of the revival of nuclear weapons in Iraq." It also noted that it had not been able to verify that Iraq had been shifting its weapons, hiding them in underground bunkers, or building mobile labs to produce biological weapons.

Their conclusions did not alter the Bush administration's mindset. Less than two weeks after the report had been presented to the UN Security Council, the United States attacked Iraq.[122]

On a couple of occasions we noted that the constitution of a decision-making group can affect the way its members use information, define a problem, survey objectives, examine the risks of possible choices, select a policy, reappraise it, and work out contingency plans.[123] In some instances, a group will have its self-appointed mind guards, rationalize collectively, develop illusions of invulnerability and unanimity, believe in its inherent morality, view other groups as adversaries and as being less capable, tolerate only self-censorship, and pressure internal dissenters to conform.[124]

The interactions between Bush and his senior foreign policy advisers reflect the symptoms captured by the "groupthink" rubric. Part of the responsibility for ensuring that the president had an opportunity to consider a range of alternatives and that the analytical process was carried out systematically, rested on the shoulders of the national security adviser. Rice failed to perform this task. One analyst referred to the NSC as "the weakest and most ineffective National Security Council in post-war American history." David Kay, who served for a while as Bush's weapons inspector in Iraq, considered Rice "the dog that did not bark."[125] It was Rice herself, however, who voiced, albeit indirectly, the most damning critique of her perform-ance as a national security adviser during the months preceding the war. On August 6, the day after Powell warned Bush that going to war against Iraq and restructuring its political system would be exception-ally complicated and costly, Rice called the secretary of state to congratulate him with the words: "That was terrific. And we need to do more of those."[126] What is conspicuous about Rice's comment is that she unintentionally acknowledged that discussion about a differ-ent option had finally taken place, more than eight months after the president had ordered the secretary of defense to start drawing up a war plan. What is troubling about her suggestion that they needed to engage in thoughtful discussions with the president about alternative options more often is that they were never carried out.

Ultimately, however, it is the president who dictates the nature of the decision-making process. Bush prided himself on allowing his top people at the White House to ask his secretary for a meeting, and on making himself available to them. "I believe the president must give people access . . . It makes my job a heck of a lot easier to be able to have access to a lot of people."[127] Such positive self-appraisal is misleading. Bush seldom demonstrated an interest in carrying out thoughtful discussions regarding available intelligence and ways to interpret a problem and resolve it; nor did he attempt to create a decision-making structure that would facilitate such a process. He showed a "disdain for contemplation or deliberation . . . a retreat from empiricism, a sometimes bullying impatience with doubters and even friendly questioners." As explained by Christopher deMuth, president of the American Enterprise Institute, a neoconservative organization, the president's senior decision-making group was "a too tightly managed decision-making process." When it made decisions, "a very small number of people [were] in the room," and this had the "effect of constricting the range of alternatives being offered."[128]

Other people who knew the president have corroborated the last construal. Paul O'Neill, who accepted the post of secretary of treasury thinking that he would be working for a president interested in looking hard for best solutions, eventually had no choice but to question his assumption. The president, acknowledged O'Neill, acted on conviction, which was crucial for success. Bush's problem, explained the former secretary of treasury, was that his action—deciding to go to war—was not "proportional to the depth of the evidence" that motivated his conviction. Bush and his closest advisers had not "thought this [the attack on Iraq] through."[129] John J. DiIulio, another senior appointee who left the White House visibly disappointed after a short tenure, concurs with O'Neill's assessment. As the person responsible for Bush's Faith-based Initiative, DiIulio had the opportunity to watch first-hand the decision-making process regarding domestic matters. "There were no actual policy white papers on domestic issues . . . [O]n social policy and related issues, the lack of even basic policy knowledge, and the only casual interest in knowing more, was somewhat breathtaking . . . Even quite junior staff would sometimes hear quite senior staff pooh-pooh any need to dig deeper for pertinent information on a given issue."[130] Even Powell, who though disturbed by the decision to go to war remained loyal to the president, repeatedly voiced concern about Bush's refusal or inability to pose probing questions and seeming failure to grasp the implications of going to war.[131] Across the Atlantic, a member of Tony Blair's cabinet was equally troubled. Robin Cook, a high-level British minister who resigned from his post over the prime minister's decision to join forces with the United States against Iraq, remarked: "Instead of using intelligence as evidence on which to base a decision about policy, we used intelligence as the basis on which to justify a policy on which we had already settled."[132] This contention was derived, in all likelihood, from information provided by the director of British military intelligence after his trip to Washington. Bush, he explained, "had made up his mind to take military action . . . But the case was thin. Saddam was not threatening his neighbors, and his WMD capability was less than that of Libya, North Korea or Iran."[133] Few understood Bush's approach to foreign policy-making better than his own national security adviser. Though conscious that one of her central functions was to ensure that Bush be exposed to quality intelligence and an array of options, she also knew that as an instinctual decision-maker who tended to view things in black and white, the president did not favor rational analyses of complex problems and tended to dismiss, almost scornfully, attempts to alter his policy after he had decided on one.[134] In short, as an outside observer proposed, the Bush administration's leading members did not view "open dialogue, based on facts . . . as something of inherent value." Dialogue based on facts, they seemed to assume, could "create doubt, which undercuts faith. It could result in a loss of confidence in the decision-maker and, just as important, *by* the decision-maker."[135]

Every foreign policy-making group that is a victim of groupthink has at least one individual who strives to ensure that only certain information or analysis reaches its core, and one who tries to protect the group's cohesion. Cheney played incessantly the role of mind guard. He repeatedly sought information that would substantiate the claim that Iraq had a nuclear weapons program in place, and he disregarded any intelligence that questioned such a conclusion. He went out of his way to try to demonstrate that there was a link between Saddam Hussein and al Qaeda, despite the absence of sound intelligence. And he ensured that those who questioned the United States's ability to transform Iraq into a viable democracy would not play a critical role in the postwar reconstruction.

The president, in turn, took it upon himself to preserve the group's unity. With his propensity to depict many aspects of human affairs as the struggle between good and evil, Bush viewed himself and the United States as the leaders of good. As the leader of the free world he felt that he needed to stand firm on his convictions and decisions. In an assessment of his discussion with Powell, in which the secretary of state had warned him about the tribulations the United States would encounter in a war against Iraq, Bush derisively dismissed any possible unease. Powell's job "is to be tactical," noted Bush. "My job is to be strategic."[136] It was Powell's task to be concerned about what could go wrong, but he, as the president, would not and could not. "I won't negotiate with myself," explained Bush. "It's that simple. If someone comes to me with a plan . . . and they have a significant amount of political backing, I'll sit down with them—talk it out. But until then, it's a closed issue."[137] He could not yield because he had to be "the calcium of the backbone. If I weaken, the whole team weakens. If I am doubtful, I can assure you there will be lots of doubts. If my confidence level in our ability declines, it will send ripples throughout the whole organization. I mean, it's essential that we be confident and determined and united . . . I don't need people around me who are not steady . . ."[138] He more or less conveyed this message to Powell when, after telling the secretary of state that he would soon order the attack on Iraq, he said: "I want you with me . . . Time to put on your uniform." Powell, who disliked being placed "in the refrigerator"— that is, not being part of the core group—complied.[139]

In sum, in an uncertain world environment foreign policy-makers, informed by partial and unreliable intelligence, are expected to be mindful of their assumptions, beliefs, and convictions. Though a few competing ideas were articulated prior to Bush's final decision to invade Iraq, the president showed little interest in listening to those who did not concur with his outlook. Impelled by the belief that his mission as leader of the United States was to propagate freedom and that to succeed he had to exercise presidential power decisively, without ever expressing self-doubt, Bush either ignored intelligence that challenged his core assumptions or took on an optimistic attitude even when the information on hand did not warrant it. His propensity to think about issues ideologically, his reluctance to try to disassemble complex problems, and his craving for action and solutions had two effects. They weakened whatever motivation some advisers might have had to engage in systematic analyses, while they swayed those with an ideologically based political agenda to promote their cause aggressively.

In a major indictment of the U.S. intelligence community, the Commission on the Intelligence Capabilities of the United States Regarding Weapons of Mass Destruction wrote that at one point the premises that directed analyses "stopped being working hypotheses and became more or less unrebuttable conclusions: worse, the intelligence system became too willing to find confirmations of them in evidence that should have been recognized at the time to be of dubious reliability. Collectors and analysts too readily accepted any evidence that supported their theory that Iraq had stockpiles and was developing weapons programs, and they explained away or simply disregarded evidence that pointed out in that direction."[140] This condemnation applies equally as well to President Bush and his closest advisers. With the exception of Secretary of State Powell, none of the other central foreign policy makers ever questioned their initial assumptions and repeatedly disregarded information that could have disputed their soundness.

CHAPTER SIX

THE ABSENCE OF A RATIONAL
PROCESS

Introduction

Structural theories are designed to explain a state's foreign policy
without reference to the thinking and actions of its decision-makers.
Analysts who focus on the structure of the international system
contend that the way power is distributed in an anarchical global or
regional system robs foreign policy-makers of much of their executive authority. Those who concentrate on the internal characteristics of
a state are not of one mind as to which domestic dimension is the chief
perpetrator. One group places the emphasis on the nature of a state's
political regime, another on its economic and class configuration,
whereas a third on its culture.[1]

This study was not crafted with the intent of casting doubts on the
import of either type of structural perspective. It acknowledges that
the international setting or a state's domestic features can affect,
separately or jointly, an actor's international behavior. But it also
contends that neither structure is so invasive that, regardless of the
circumstances, it invariably leaves foreign policy-makers with only
one choice. President Franklin Roosevelt had no choice but to
respond militarily to Japan's surprise attack on Pearl Harbor in
December 1941. Failure on his part to do so would have undermined
both the power and prestige of the United States in the world arena,
and would have enraged the American people and Congress.
Conversely, in 1991 and 2003, the first and second Bush administrations could have opted not to go to war against Iraq. In neither

instance did the international setting or the U.S. domestic environment compel them to resort to war. To understand their decisions, thus, this study sought to unravel the way each president and his advisers came to the decision that armed conflict against Iraq would be the optimum solution.

Most contemporary theories of foreign policy-making lack parsimony. Confounded by the wide array of factors that can shape the foreign policy-making process, a number of analysts initially strove to identify them, and to explain the way they affected decisions. Others tried to build on the initial works by aggregating the assumed effects generated by organizational and cognitive factors and then molding them into quasi-parsimonious foreign policy-making theories. Wary of the diagnostic missteps that could result by the moving from the first type of analysis to the second one without first isolating the actual features at play in the foreign policy-making process, this study positions both approaches under the same tent. Via the analyses of two surprise attacks and two acts of war, it identified the various elements that encroached on the two Bush administrations' foreign policy-making processes, and generated some tentative generalizations. This chapter, by means of a comparative analysis of each Bush administration's foreign policy-making process, retrieves the various nets cast and encapsulates the resulting conclusions in the form of a theoretical construct.

Impediments to Rationality

Rationality in foreign policy-making is an uncommon trait. Its impediments are multiple, and can be categorized according to their sources and nature.

Groupthink

As noted in chapter one, the nature of a decision-making group can shape the manner in which its members use information, characterize a problem, review objectives, consider the risks of alternative choices, and choose a policy.

Groupthink always has a root. Its principal originator can be a stressful situation, the group's leading figures, or a combination of both. In the case of both Bush administrations, it was self-generated. The first Bush administration, upon positioning U.S. forces on Saudi territory, could have opted for a policy of containment—an alternative that, while calling for patience, would have induced manageable stress. Likewise, the second Bush had choices besides resorting to war to lessen the threat evoked by Saddam Hussein's erratic behavior. If any stress was generated during the second case, it was induced by the Bush administration's initial caustic decision to ask the UN Security Council to investigate whether Saddam Hussein's regime had developed or was developing WMD, the vain attempts by the UN inspectors to find the alleged weapons' arsenal, and the extensive deployment of U.S. forces poised to invade Iraq as the inspections ensued.

A leader with a specific political agenda will sometimes engender a groupthink environment to advance his preferred policy. In the first Bush administration, the president and his national security adviser, determined to adopt a belligerent posture vis-à-vis Saddam Hussein, created a rather rigid decision-making hierarchy by dealing with its members according to their status and field of expertise. Though Powell and a few of the other members of the inner circle believed that going to war against Iraq should be delayed until containment had been given a fair chance to achieve its intended goal, they did not dare to stand up and be counted. They lacked the nerve to say: "I think that it would be wrong to resort to war without first giving containment the time to force Saddam Hussein to recognize that it would be in his and his country's interests to pull the Iraqi forces out of Kuwait."[2]

The reluctance to be a contrarian is not uncommon. Theodore Sorensen, who worked closely with President John F. Kennedy, wrote that even "the most distinguished and forthright adviser is usually reluctant to stand alone. If he fears his persistence in a meeting will earn him disapprobation of his colleagues, a rebuff by the President . . . he may quickly seek the safety of the greater numbers."[3]

Irving Janis, in turn, explained that in instances in which the disparity in status and power between the decision-makers is substantial, it is up to the leader to ensure that neither acts as a barrier to the articulation of dissenting opinions.[4]

The first President Bush refused to create a decision-making atmosphere that fostered the open expression and exchange of rival opinions on two occasions—when he decided to use force against Iraq to expel its forces from Kuwait, and when he decided to bring the war to an end instead of marching toward Baghdad to topple Saddam Hussein's regime. The second President Bush and his closest advisers inflicted groupthink on their core decision-making group in a markedly more potent way.

When data is incomplete and inadequate, and when analysts differ as to the inferences they should derive from it, groupthink facilitates the creation of a cohesive vision with respect to what the information denotes. In spite of the fact that UN inspectors and some of the intelligence agencies, both in the United States and Britain, doubted Saddam Hussein had developed or was trying to develop WMD, and that they had been unable to determine whether the Iraqi leader and al Qaeda had worked together, the second President Bush, Cheney, and Rice created a decision-making environment wherein it became very difficult for the others members of the inner group to challenge the assertion that both scenarios had become, or were about to become, a reality in Iraq. The deep reluctance to challenge the assumptions that guided the decision-making process carried over into the intelligence community. "Well before March 2003," writes the former national intelligence officer for the Near East and South Asia at the CIA Paul Pillar, "intelligence analysts ... knew ... that the Bush administration would frown or ignore analysis that called into question a decision to go to war and welcome analysis that supported such a decision ... Intelligence analysts felt a strong wind consistently blowing in one direction ... It may not be possible to point to one key instance of such bending or to measure the cumulative effect of such pressure. But the effect was probably significant."[5]

Two Presidents—Relatively Similar Approaches
to Decision-Making

In their respective foreign policy-making environments, the two presidents shared two distinct, and critical, traits—a willingness to rely on their instincts when formulating a decision, and a penchant to use moral language to validate their choice.

The first president, in spite of, or maybe because of, his far-reaching foreign policy knowledge, responded to the Iraqi invasion of Kuwait in a visceral way. As explained by his own secretary of state, James Baker, instead of conducting a thorough assessment of options, Bush instinctively decided that he would not tolerate Saddam Hussein's act of aggression against Kuwait and that he would rely on military force if necessary in order to achieve his goal. Bush's son, even though he did not possess his father's expertise on international affairs, relied on a similar approach to conclude that the United States would depose Saddam Hussein and replace his regime with a democratic one. He was untroubled by the absence of reliable information, and he disregarded the need to consider a range of options, predict their possible consequences, and assess which one would most likely bring about the best result. His instinct told him that going to war in order to liberate Iraq was the correct decision.

The two presidents validated their reliance on their instincts with the claim that their actions were morally sound. The first president defined the struggle with Saddam Hussein as a battle between good and evil. The second envisaged the United States as a liberator, an actor whose principal task as the world's prime power was to propagate "God's gift to the world"—freedom.

Foreign policy-makers, mainly those with some knowledge of history, are often captives of the past.[6] The lessons they infer from previous occurrences typically dictate the way they interpret and respond to a new international problem. In the process, however, analogies can mask aspects of the present case that, under closer inspection, might reveal differences from the past one.[7] A number of historical events and their respective lessons were very much in the minds of the leading members of the first Bush administration. For Scowcroft, and especially for the first President Bush, the central analogy was Munich. From the 1938 debacle they inferred that appeasement never pacifies tyrants. Because Saddam Hussein was another Adolf Hitler, hence evil, the United States had no choice but to respond aggressively to the Iraqi leader's actions. In turn, the problems the U.S. forces had encountered in Panama as they sought to capture its military strongman Manuel Noriega helped convince the two U.S. leaders that marching into Baghdad with the intent of overthrowing the Saddam Hussein regime was not a workable option.

The Pentagon's military officers had their own distinct analogies— Vietnam and Lebanon. Led by the chairman of the Chiefs of Staff, those responsible for planning the operation viewed the two cases as examples of the types of mistakes the U.S. military could not afford to repeat. In both instances, U.S. policy-makers had assumed that if their country applied force gradually the enemy would seek a diplomatic solution at an early level of escalation. In due course they concluded that they had been wrong, and that the enemy had used gradualism as an opportunity to augment its own military and political power. The lesson: if the United States must fight a war with a Third World entity, it must use as much firepower as necessary to destroy swiftly its adversary's fighting capability and will.

Members of the second Bush administration also reasoned analogically. Its central figure, with his inadequate international political experience and limited knowledge of history, assumed that the United States' success at transforming Germany and Japan after World War II would be replicated in Iraq. To define the challenge posed by Saddam Hussein's regime and to design a policy that would address it, however, Bush did not need to turn his eyes to the distant past. The events of September 11, 2001 convinced him that despite the absence of solid information about Saddam Hussein's intentions and policies toward the United States, he could not afford to assume that they would be benign. September 11 also affected the way the president's national security adviser interpreted the threat generated by the Iraqi leader.

Those with more solid international resumes, such as Vice President Cheney and Paul Wolfowitz, could not forget how poorly they had read Iraq and its leader when they served under the first President Bush. Their failure to predict the Iraqi attack on Kuwait, along with the subsequent discovery of WMD, including a clandestine nuclear program, by the members of UN Special Commission and the IAEA, convinced both that Saddam Hussein was a deceitful leader who, in all likelihood, had renewed his weapons buildup program following the departure of the weapons inspectors in 1998. The CIA director George Tenet shared their concern. Saddam Hussein had deceived the United States once, and he would try to do it again. Moreover, Wolfowitz, like the first President Bush, perceived Saddam Hussein as another Hitler, and feared that if Washington did not destroy the Iraqi leader's regime, the United States would be repeating the same mistake made by those who failed to act forcefully against Hitler during his early drive to reinvigorate Germany's power.

Part of this book's argument has been that a readiness to reflect on alternative options and a willingness to reevaluate one's original decision before it is finally implemented are essential to rational decision-making. This kind of process is sometimes undermined by a president who is impatient and takes it as a mark of character to act decisively and to stand by his initial decision. Of the two Bush presidents, only the second one consistently disregarded Liddell Harts's insightful counsel that a leader must have "unlimited patience."[8] Each President Bush, moreover, was determined to make sure that no one questioned his personal courage and willingness to do the "right thing."

The first one expressed this sentiment when he noted at the end of the year 1990 that he would not change his mind; he was prepared to go to war to liberate Kuwait even if the American public and the entire Congress opposed his decision. His son, in addition to lacking the kind of patience leaders ought to have before engaging their state in war, sought to project his strength of mind in a particularly unique way. As noted by a political leader who had observed the second President Bush closely, and as corroborated by the president himself, his leadership style bordered on the hurried and was constantly demanding immediate action and solutions. Equally as important, the second President Bush believed that one of his main obligations as leader of the United States during a time of crisis was to act as his administration's "calcium of the backbone." To succeed against Iraq, his administration had to project an image of confidence, determination, and unity. Any hesitation or sign of frailty on his part would lessen his advisers' tenacity and signal to the various organizations responsible for implementing the foreign policy of the United States that the president questioned his own policy. Therefore, instead of striving to analyze a decision thoroughly and viewing the reconsideration of his initial decision as an attempt to reduce the likelihood that he and his advisers had overlooked workable options and consequences, the second President Bush viewed both forms of behavior as signs of weakness.

A Unified Perspective

In different stages of the study we demonstrated that the "noncompensatory" strategy of decision-making is a markedly more valuable explanatory model than the "compensatory" approach. Specifically, we showed that each administration, rather than comparing the extent to which the positive dimensions of a small number of pertinent alternatives compensated its negative elements, stressed in every instance the positive factor of its preferred policy and the negative components of other options. The first Bush administration opted for this type of decision-making strategy when it dismissed warnings from its intelligence analysts that Iraq was about to attack Kuwait, and when it decided to use force to expel the Iraqi forces from Kuwait and then to not invade Iraq. The second one replicated the approach when it refused to acknowledge the strong possibility that a non-state actor such as al Qaeda would launch a direct attack on U.S. territory, and when it chose to invade Iraq in order to bring down Saddam Hussein's government and replace it with a democratic one.

Epilogue

A few months after the U.S. forces had marched into Baghdad, President George W. Bush claimed that the United States had accomplished its mission in Iraq. Two years later, in May 2005, a U.S. senior officer in Baghdad said, during a background briefing, that victory in Iraq was not assured. He emphasized that though it was likely that the United States would succeed, "it could still fail."[9]

The change in interpretation is revealing in two important ways. First, it reaffirms our earlier contention that the younger President Bush tended to render judgment hastily. An introspective leader would have kept in mind Clausewitz's warning that war is the province of chance—one that "increases the uncertainty of every circumstance and deranges the course of events." Clearly, that was not the way the second Bush administration approached the war against Iraq. As noted by Secretary of the Army Thomas E. White, the Pentagon's working budgetary assumption was that 90 days after the completion of the operation, which entailed the defeat of the Iraqi forces, the United States would withdraw the first 50,000 and then every 30 days it would take out another 50,000 until everybody was back. By the middle of 2006, it was unquestionable that the fighting in Iraq had lasted longer, had been more intense, and had been costlier, both from a human and a material perspective, than initially estimated.

Second, it underscores our earlier contention that though complete rationality in foreign policy-making is humanly impossible, a substantial measure of rationality is greatly needed. The presence of rationality in an uncertain world cannot guarantee success, but its repeated absence courts disaster. And yet, it is unclear whether even a modicum of rationality is viable in the sphere of foreign policy-making. George Orwell warned that politics, more than any other field of human endeavor, is less an instrument for expressing thought than a means for "preventing thought."[10] As explained by Jon Elster, the physical processes that underlie strong emotions and craving invariably undermine rationality.[11] Little of what we presented in this book gives us reason to think that their pessimistic outlook was unwarranted.

NOTES

Introduction Two Surprises, Two Wars, Two Presidents, One Family

1. A fourth plane crashed in a field in Pennsylvania.
2. Morgenthau acknowledged that foreign policy-makers have not always been rational, objective, and unemotional, and that in democracies they have not always been successful at preventing popular emotions from impairing the rationality of foreign policy. See Hans Morgenthau, *Politics Among Nations*. Revised by Kenneth W. Thompson (New York: Alfred A. Knopf, 1985), 7.
3. For a useful discussion of the explanatory strengths and weaknesses of realism, see Stephen D. Krasner, *Defending the National Interest* (Princeton: Princeton University Press, 1978), 41.

Chapter One Alternative Theories of Foreign Policy-Making

1. Morgenthau, *Politics Among Nations*, 5–7.
2. Bruce Bueno de Mesquita and David Lalman, "Domestic Opposition and Foreign War," *American Political Science Review* 84 (1990): 750.
3. Bueno de Mesquita, "Forecasting Political Decisions: An Expected Utility Approach to Post-Khomeini Iran," *PS: Political Science and Politics* 17 (1984):228. Not everyone accepts this definition of rationality. As Frank Zagare notes, the concept of rationality can be either procedural or instrumental. Procedural rationality, which has been articulated by scholars as diverse as Herbert Simon, Sidney Verba, and Graham Allison, focuses on the actual decision-making process. According to this perspective, a rational decision-maker is one who, when confronted with a problem that requires a solution, gathers information, ranks his values, assesses a number of alternatives and the risks he is likely to encounter in the implementation of each one, and makes a choice guided by his want to maximize his returns. Instrumental rationality is similar to that depicted by Bueno de Mesquita. More specifically, it refers to the process of imposing connected and transitive

preferences over a set of available outcomes. Under this definition, any individual confronted with two or more alternatives that give rise to different outcomes will select the one that yields his preferred outcome. As Christopher Achen and Duncan Snidal have explained, this view of rationality refers to choices, not to mental calculations. See Frank C. Zagare, "Rationality and Deterrence," *World Politics*, vol. 42, no. 2 (January 1990): 239–40. See also Christopher Achen and Duncan Snidal, "Rational Deterrence Theory and Comparative Case Studies," *World Politics*, vol. 41, no. 2 (January 1989): 164. For a critique of instrumental rationality, see Alex Roberto Hybel, *Power Over Rationality: The Bush Administration and the Gulf Crisis* (Albany, NY: State University of New York Press, 1993), 17–19 and 106–7.

4. See Alexander L. George, *Presidential Decisionmaking in Foreign Policy: The Effective Use of Information and Advice* (Boulder, CO: Westview Press, 1979), 73–4.

5. Ibid., 112–3.

6. Jean A. Garrison, *Games Advisors Play—Foreign Policy in the Nixon and Carter Administrations* (College Station, Texas: Texas A & M University Press, 1999), xx.

7. Irving L. Janis, *Victims of Groupthink* (Boston: Houghton Mifflin, 1972), 9.

8. See Alex Roberto Hybel, *Power Over Rationality*, 27.

9. Herbert Simon, *Models of Man* (New York: John Wiley and Sons, 1957).

10. Charles F. Hartmann's work remains the pioneering study on the stress-inducing effects of international crises on foreign policy-making. See Hartmann, *Crises in Foreign Policy: A Simulation Analysis* (Indianapolis: Bobbs-Merrill, 1969).

11. See Alex Roberto Hybel, *How Leaders Reason: U.S. Intervention in the Caribbean Basin and Latin America* (Oxford: Basil Blackwell, 1990), 22; and Deborah Welch Larson, *Origins of Containment* (Princeton: Princeton University Press, 1985), 34–7.

12. See Hybel, *Power Over Rationality*, 22–3; Hybel, *How Leaders Reason*, 6–8; and Larson, *Origins of Containment*, 50–7. The literature on the use of historical analogies by policy-makers is extensive. Here only some of the best-known works are identified. Ernest May, *"Lessons" of the Past. The Use and Misuse of History in American Foreign Policy* (New York: Oxford University Press, 1973); Robert Jervis, *Perceptions and Misperceptions in International Politics* (Princeton: Princeton University Press, 1976); Richard E. Neustadt and Ernest R. May, *Thinking in Time: The Uses of History by Decision Makers* (New York: The Free Press, 1986); Scot Macdonald, *Rolling the Dice. Historical Analogies and Decisions to Use Military Force in Regional Contingencies* (New York: Greenwood Press, 2000); and Jeffrey Record, *Making History, Thinking*

History: Munich, Vietnam, and Presidential Uses of Forces from Korea to Kosovo (Annapolis, MD: Naval Institute Press, 2002).

13. Hybel, *How Leaders Reason*, 22.
14. For a more extensive discussion of attribution theory, schema theory, and cognitive consistency theory, see ibid., chapter 2.
15. See George, *Presidential Decisionmaking*, chapter 8; and John P. Burke and Fred I. Greenstein, *How Presidents Test Reality* (New York: Russell Sage Foundation, 1991), 23.
16. See Charles W. Ostrom Jr., and Brian Job, "The President and the Political Use of Force," *American Political Science Review*, 80 (1986): 541–66; and Bueno de Mesquita and Lalman, "Domestic Opposition, and Foreign War," 747–65.
17. Alex Mintz, "The Decision to Attack Iraq: A Noncompensatory Theory of Decision Making," *Journal of Conflict Resolution*, vol. 37, no. 4 (December 1993): 598.
18. See Amos Tversky and Daniel Kahneman, "The Framing of a Decision and the Psychology of Choice," *Science*, vol. 211 (January 1981): 453–8.

Chapter Two   Two Harmful Surprises

1. See Majid Khadduri and Edmund Ghareeb, *War in the Gulf, 1990–1991. The Iraq-Kuwait Conflict and its Implications* (New York: Oxford University Press, 1997), 98. See also Lawrence Freedman and Ephraim Karsh, *The Gulf Conflict, 1990–1991* (Princeton: Princeton University Press, 1993), 26–7.
2. Khadduri and Ghareeb, *War in the Gulf*, 98–9.
3. Quoted in "Kuwait: How the West Blundered," in *The Gulf War Reader*, ed. Micah L. Sifry and Christopher Cerf (New York: Random House, 1991), 100.
4. See ibid., 102.
5. Quoted in Bob Woodward, *The Commanders* (New York: Simon and Schuster, 1991), 201.
6. Khadduri and Ghareeb, *War in the Gulf*, 100–1.
7. See John Bulloch and Harvey Morris, *Saddam's War: The Origins of the Kuwait Conflict and the International Response* (London: Faber and Faber, 1991), 101.
8. It should be kept in mind that by the time Iraq and Iran went to war, a new regime had assumed power in Tehran.
9. See Khadduri and Ghareeb, *War in the Gulf*, 85.
10. See ibid., 79–87 and 105.
11. See ibid., 106–7.
12. Walter P. Lang and CIA analysts were initially perplexed by this move. They could not understand why Saddam Hussein would redeploy his

forces to the west and risk an Israeli attack. This lack of understanding seems to indicate that the analysts were unaware that Saddam Hussein had been reassured by the Bush administration that Israel had no intention of attacking Iraq.

13. See "U.S. Policy Toward the Persian Gulf," *National Security Directive 26*. Secret (Washington, DC: October 2, 1989).

14. George Bush and Brent Scowcroft, *A World Transformed* (New York: Alfred Knopf, 1998), 307.

15. Quoted in Woodward, *The Commanders*, 210.

16. Janice Gross Stein, "Threat-Based Strategies of Conflict Management: Why Did They Fail in the Gulf?" in *The Political Psychology of the Gulf War*, ed. Stanley A. Renshon (Pittsburgh: University of Pittsburgh Press, 1993), 123.

17. Brian Shellum, *A Chronology of Defense Intelligence in the Gulf War: A Research Aid for Analysts* (Washington, DC: DIA History Office, 1997).

18. Colin Powell, "The Gulf War: An Oral History," *PBS Frontline*. Available from http://www.pbs.org/wgbh/pages/frontilnegulf/oral/powell/1.html, accessed February 23, 2004.

19. Richard Haass, "The Gulf War: An Oral History," *PBS: Frontline*. Available from http://www.pbs.org/wgbh/pages/frontilne'gulf/oral/haass/5.html, accessed February 23, 2004.

20. See Stein, "Threat-Based Strategies," 124.

21. See Khadduri and Ghareeb, *War in the Gulf*, 11.

22. All the quotes and interpretations come directly from the transcript of the meeting, as released by Baghdad. See "The Glaspie Transcript," in *The Iraq War Reader*, ed. Micah L. Sifry and Christopher Cerf (New York: Simon and Schuster, 2003), 61–71.

23. Glaspie was particularly critical of Diane Sawyer's program on ABC. "What happened in the program," said the U.S. ambassador to Saddam Hussein "was cheap and unjust. And this is the real picture of what happens in the American media—even to American politicians themselves." See ibid., 67.

24. This passage reinforces our previous contention that the United States had been monitoring closely Saddam Hussein's and his foreign minister's earlier speeches and letters.

25. Quoted in Steve A. Yetiv, *The Persian Gulf Crisis* (Westport, CT: Greenwood Press, 1997), 9.

26. See interviews of Powell and Haas, "The Gulf War: An Oral History."

27. Michael J. Mazarr, Don M. Snider, and James A. Blackwell, Jr., *Desert Storm—The Gulf War and What We Learned* (Boulder, CO: Westview Press, 1993), 40.

28. Quoted in Freedman and Karsh, *The Gulf Conflict*, 6.

29. Bush and Scowcroft, *A World Transformed*, 302; see also Brent Scowcrfot, "The Gulf War: An Oral History," *PBS Frontline*. Available from

http://www.pbs.org/wgbh/pages/frontilne'gulf/oral/scowcroft/1.html, accessed February 23, 2004.

30. See Scowcroft, "The Gulf War: An Oral History."
31. Yetiv, *The Persian Gulf Crisis*, 10.
32. Shellum, *A Chronology of Defense Intelligence in the Gulf War*.
33. Quoted in Woodward, *The Commanders*, 216–17
34. Shellum, *A Chronology of Defense Intelligence in the Gulf War*.
35. See "Kuwait: How the West Blundered," 104.
36. Richard A. Clarke, *Against All Enemies: Inside America's War on Terror*. (New York: Simon & Schuster, 2004), 56.
37. Mazarr, Snider, and Blackwell, Jr., *Desert Storm*, 40.
38. Ibid., 43.
39. Powell, "The Gulf War: An Oral History."
40. Haass, "The Gulf War: An Oral History."
41. Bush and Scowcroft, *A World Transformed*, 302.
42. Ibid., 302.
43. Shellum, *A Chronology of Defense Intelligence in the Gulf War*.
44. See Condoleezza Rice, "Promoting the National Interest," *Foreign Affairs*, vol. 79, no. 1, (January/February 2000), 45–62. Paradoxically, though Rice's argument delineated the foreign policy agenda the new Bush administration sought to implement prior to September 11, the president never read Rice's piece. Bush acknowledged this much during a press conference held January 26, 2005. See also Chris J. Dolan, "Foreign Policy on the Offensive," in *Striking First—The Preventive War Doctrine and the Reshaping of U.S. Foreign Policy*, ed. Betty Glad and Chris J. Dolan (New York: Palgrave Macmillan, 2004), 11.
45. Quoted in *The 9/11 Commission Report* (New York: W. W. Norton, 2004), 199.
46. See Bob Woodward, *Plan of Attack* (New York: Simon and Schuster, 2004), 12.
47. Clarke, *Against All Enemies*, 227. See also *The 9/11 Commission Report*, 199; and Michael Elliot, "Could 9/11 Have Been Prevented?" *Time*, August 4, 2002.
48. Richard Clarke, *Memorandum for Condoleezza Rice. Subject: Presidential Policy Initiative/Review—The Al-Qida Network*. (Washington, DC: National Security Council January 25, 2001).
49. See *The 9/11 Commission Report*, 201.
50. Ibid., 203.
51. Clarke, *Against All Enemies*, 231.
52. *The 9/11 Commission Report*, 205–13.
53. Clarke, *Against All Enemies*, 97.
54. *The 9/11 Commission Report*, 209–10. See also Clarke, *Against All Enemies*, 254.
55. Anonymous, *Imperial Hubris* (Washington, DC: Brassey's, 2004), 22–3.

56. Ibid., x–xi.
57. In the article, bin Laden remarks, "[N]o one argues today about three facts that are known to everyone." Text of "Fatawa Urging Jihad Against Americans," *Al-Quds al'Arab* in Arabic, February 23, 1998, 3.
58. Ibid.
59. Anonymous, *Imperial Hubris*, 23–4.
60. *The 9/11 Commission Report*, 255.
61. Ibid.
62. Ibid., 256; and Clarke, *Against All Enemies*, 235.
63. Clarke, *Against All Enemies*, 236.
64. Bob Woodward, *Bush at War* (New York: Simon and Schuster, 2002), 4.
65. *The 9/11 Commission Report*, 257.
66. Ibid.
67. Ibid.
68. Ibid., 258–9.
69. A copy of the memo can be found in note 75. See Elliot, "Could 9/11 Have Been Prevented?"
70. Details of the plot have not been declassified.
71. Quotes appear in *The 9/11 Commission Report*, 259.
72. Ibid., 260.
73. Ibid., 259–60.
74. See August 6, 2001, PDB in *The 9/11 Commission Report*, 261.
75. *The 9/11 Commission Report*, 260–2.

Declassified and Approved
for Release, 10 April 2004

Bin Ladin Determined To Strike in US

Clandestine, foreign government, and media reports indicate Bin Ladin since 1997 has wanted to conduct terrorist attacks in the US. Bin Ladin implied in US television interviews in 1997 and 1998 that his followers would follow the example of World Trade Center bomber Ramzi Yousef and "bring the fighting to America."

After US missile strikes on his base in Afghanistan in 1998, Bin Ladin told followers he wanted to retaliate in Washington, according to a service.

An Egyptian Islamic Jihad (EIJ) operative told an service at the same time that Bin Ladin was planning to exploit the operative's access to the US to mount a terrorist strike.

The millennium plotting in Canada in 1999 may have been part of Bin Ladin's first serious attempt to implement a terrorist strike in the US. Convicted plotter Ahmed Ressam has told the FBI that he conceived the idea to attack Los Angeles International Airport himself, but that Bin Ladin lieutenant Abu Zubaydah encouraged him and helped facilitate the operation. Ressam also said that in 1998 Abu Zubaydah was planning his own US attack.

Ressam says Bin Ladin was aware of the Los Angeles operation.

Although Bin Ladin has not succeeded, his attacks against the US Embassies in Kenya and Tanzania in 1998 demonstrate that he prepares operations years in advance and is not deterred by setbacks. Bin Ladin associates surveilled our Embassies in Nairobi and Dar es Salaam as early as 1993, and some members of the Nairobi cell planning the bombings were arrested and deported in 1997.

Al-Qa'ida members—including some who are US citizens—have resided in or traveled to the US for years, and the group apparently maintains a support structure that could aid attacks. Two al-Qa'ida members found guilty in the conspiracy to bomb our Embassies in East Africa were US citizens, and a senior EIJ member lived in California in the mid-1990s.

A clandestine source said in 1998 that a Bin Ladin cell in New York was recruiting Muslim-American youth for attacks.

We have not been able to corroborate some of the more sensational threat reporting, such as that from a service in 1998 saying that Bin Ladin wanted to hijack a US aircraft to gain the release of "Blind Shaykh" 'Umar 'Abd al-Rahman and other US-held extremists.

— Nevertheless, FBI information since that time indicates patterns of suspicious activity in this country consistent with preparations for hijackings or other types of attacks, including recent surveillance of lederal buildings in New York.

The FBI is conducting approximately 70 full field investigations throughout the US that it considers Bin Ladin-related. CIA and the FBI are investigating a call to our Embassy in the UAE in May saying that a group of Bin Ladin supporters was in the US planning attacks with explosives.

For the President Only
6 August 2001

76. Moussaoui had begun his training in February at the Airman Flight School in Norman, Oklahoma.
77. See *The 9/11 Commission Report*, 273–6. See also Elliot, "Could 9/11 Have Been Prevented?"
78. As previously mentioned, Moussaoui was a French national, so the Paris office was an obvious choice. Furthermore, Moussaoui had lived in London as well, making the London office another meaningful target for inquiry.

79. *The 9/11 Commission Report*, 274–5.
80. Ibid., 275. London responded to the FBI request after September 11. It informed Minneapolis that Moussaoui had attended an al Qaeda training camp in Afghanistan.
81. Ibid. From Michael Elliot's report in *Time* one could infer that Tenet did not know about Moussaoui's activities, but *The 9/11 Commission Report* did not arrive at the same conclusion. The discrepancy could be explained by the fact that Elliot's piece was published some two years before *The 9/11 Commission Report*.
82. See Eric Lichtblau, "9/11 Report Cites Many Warnings About Hijacking," *The New York Times*, February 10, 2005.
83. Ibid.

Chapter Three   The Logic of Surprise versus the Logic of Surprise Avoidance

Walter P. Lang was a senior civilian intelligence analyst for the Middle East and South Asia region at the Pentagon. Quoted in Woodward, *The Commanders*, 219.
Colin Powell was the chairman, Joint Chiefs of Staff. Powell, "The Gulf War: An Oral History."
The message was intercepted by U.S. intelligence prior to September 11, 2001. Quoted in Woodward, *Bush at War*, 4.
Statement made by the senator during a conversation with CIA Director George Tenet, in the early morning of September 11, 2001. Ibid., 3.

1. See Alex Roberto Hybel, *The Logic of Surprise* MA: Lexington Books, 1986), 9.
2. Ibid., 13–4.
3. Alexander L. George and Richard Smoke, *Deterrence and American Foreign Policy* (New York: Columbia University Press, 1974), 582.
4. See Hybel, *The Logic of Surprise*, 15–16.
5. See Klaus Knorr, "Failures in National Intelligence Estimates: The Case of the Cuban Missile Crisis," *World Politics*, vol. 16, no. 1 (April 1964): 459.
6. Quoted in Freedman and Karsh, *The Gulf Conflict*, 59.
7. See Bruce W. Jentleson, *American Foreign Policy* (New York: W. W. Norton, 2004), 376.
8. Lou Cannon, *President Reagan. The Role of a Lifetime* (New York: Simon and Schuster, 1991), 604.
9. *Report of the President's Special Review Board [Tower Report]*, 1987, B-4.
10. Casper Weinberger, *Fighting for Peace: Seven Critical Years in the Pentagon* (New York: Warner Books, 1990), 363–4.
11. Cannon, *President Reagan*, 605.
12. Quoted in Hybel, *Power Over Rationality*, 49–50.

13. Jochen Hippler, "Iraq's Military Power: The German Connection," *Middle East Report* (January–February 1991): 27–31.
14. Kendal Stiles, *Case Histories in International Politics* (New York: Pearson, 2004), 137.
15. Scowcroft, "The Gulf War: An Oral History."
16. James Baker, "The Gulf War: An Oral History." *PBS Frontline.* Available from http://www.pbs.org/wgbh/pages/frontline/gulf/oral/baker/1.html, accessed February 23, 2003.
17. Janice Gross Stein, "Military Deception, Strategic Surprise, and Conventional Discourse: A Political Analysis of Egypt and Israel, 1971–1973," *The Journal of Strategic Studies*, vol. 5, no. 1 (March 1982): 92–121.
18. Powell, "The Gulf War: An Oral History."
19. Ibid. For a discussion as to whether deterrence is a viable policy against tyrants, see Betty Glad, "Can Tyrants be Deterred?" in Glad and Dolan, eds., *Striking First*, 58–9.
20. Scowcroft, "The Gulf War: Oral History."
21. Haass, "The Gulf War: An Oral History."
22. One can also apply the notions of *tenacity* and *status quo bias* to explain the unwillingness on the part of the first President Bush and his advisers to give serious consideration to the idea that Saddam Hussein was preparing to invade Kuwait. Charles Pierce has argued that there are four ways of "fixing knowledge." One of them, *tenacity*, refers to an individual's stubborn refusal to entertain ideas that might contradict the one he values. The individual declines to examine information dispassionately and, instead, chooses arbitrarily the kind of information that is likely to induce a comforting feeling. See Charles Sanders Pierce, "The Fixation of Belief," in *The Essential Pierce, vol. 1*, ed. N. Houser and C. Kloesel (Bloomington, IN: Indiana University Press, 1992), 109–23. Original work published in 1877. Also of significant value is the *status quo bias* concept, which refers to the tendency to prefer an existing state of affairs to alternative ones. See Raquel Fernandez and Doni Rodrik, "Resistance to Reform: Status Quo Bias in the Presence of Individual Specific Uncertainty," *American Economic Review*, vol. 81 (December 1991): 1146–55. I am grateful to Stuart Vyse, a colleague in the Psychology Department at Connecticut College, for pointing out the two concepts.
23. Haas, "The Gulf War: An Oral History."
24. *The 9/11 Commission Report* distinguished between human intelligence and signals intelligence: "[V]irtually all the information regarding possible domestic threats came from human sources. The information on overseas threats came mainly from signals intelligence. Officials believed that signals intelligence was more reliable than human intelligence." *The 9/11 Commission Report*, 535.
25. See Elliot, "Could 9/11 Have Been Prevented?"

26. See Bueno de Mesquita, "Forecasting Policy Decisions," 226–36.
27. Mintz, "Decision to Attack Iraq," 596–7.
28. Ibid., 598.
29. Quoted in Stein, "Threat-Based Strategies," 130. Quoted also in Freedman and Karsh, *The Gulf Conflict*, 58.
30. Ron Suskind, *The Price of Loyalty* (New York: Simon and Schuster, 2004), 126.
31. See Clarke, *Against All Enemies*, 226.

Chapter Four Two Very Different Wars

1. Karl von Clausewitz, "On the Nature of War," in *Classics of International Relations*, ed. John A. Vasquez (Englewood Cliffs, NJ: Prentice-Hall, 1990), 295.
2. Freedman and Karsh, *The Gulf Conflict*, 85.
3. In all likelihood such a discussion did not ensue because shortly after Washington had learned about the invasion, CIA and Department of State representatives met with the head of the Saudi intelligence to find out whether Saudi Arabia would welcome U.S. troops. The Saudi representative was noncommittal. See ibid., 86.
4. Bush and Scowcroft, *A World Transformed*, 3.
5. Ibid., 318.
6. Ibid., 322.
7. Stephen J. Wayne, "President Bush Goes to War: A Psychological Interpretation from a Distance," in *The Political Psychology of the Gulf War*, ed. Renshon, 33.
8. Freedman and Karsh, *The Gulf Conflict*, 76.
9. Ibid., 81.
10. Quoted in James P. Pfiffner, "Presidential Policy-Making and the Gulf War," in *The Presidency and the Persian Gulf War*, ed. Marcia Lynn Whicker, James P. Pfiffner and Raymond A. Moore (Westport, CT: Praeger, 1993), 3.
11. Bush and Scowcroft, *A World Transformed*, 323.
12. Ibid.
13. Freedman and Karsh, *The Gulf Conflict*, 76.
14. Powell, "The Gulf War: An Oral History."
15. As told by Brent Scowcroft to Yetiv on June 26, 1996. See Yetiv, *The Persian Gulf Crisis*, 64 and 80 (endnote 15).
16. Eagleburger offered this interpretation to Steve A. Yetiv during an interview on July 23, 1996. See ibid., 63 and 80 (endnote 14).
17. Freedman and Karsh, *The Gulf Conflict*, 87.
18. Quoted in Pfiffner, "Presidential Policy-Making," 4.
19. Colin Powell, *My American Journey* (New York: Random House, 1995), 480.

20. Hybel, *Power Over Rationality*, 62–3; see also Freedman and Karsh, *The Gulf Conflict*, 87–8.
21. Quoted in Pfiffner, "Presidential Policy-Making and the Gulf War," 4.
22. Hybel, *Power Over Rationality*, 63.
23. Quoted in ibid., 63.
24. Khadduri and Ghareeb, *War in the Gulf*, 132.
25. See Mazarr, Snider, and Blackwell, Jr., *Desert Storm*, 53.
26. Quoted in Freedman and Karsh, *The Gulf Conflict*, 90.
27. See ibid., 91.
28. Robert J. Spitzer, "The Conflict Between Congress and the President Over War," in *The Presidency and the Persian Gulf War*, ed. Marcia Lynn Whicker, James P. Pfiffner and Raymond A. Moore (Westport, CT: Praeger, 1993), 28.
29. Quoted in Freedman and Karsh, *The Gulf Conflict*, 93.
30. Woodward, *The Commanders*, 320.
31. Quoted in Yetiv, *The Persian Gulf Crisis*, 64.
32. Woodward, *The Commanders*, 191, 255.
33. Ibid., 255.
34. Powell, "The Gulf War: An Oral History."
35. See David Halberstam, *War in Time of Peace* (New York: Scribner, 2001), 47–52; and Freedman and Karsh, *The Gulf Conflict*, 203.
36. Freedman and Karsh, *The Gulf Conflict*, 202–3.
37. Quoted in ibid., 204.
38. Quoted in Hybel, *Power Over Rationality*, 72–3. See also Yetiv, *The Persian Gulf Crisis*, 65.
39. Woodward, *The Commanders*, 320.
40. See Yetiv, *The Persian Gulf Crisis*, 64; and Hybel, *Power Over Rationality*, 72.
41. Quoted in Yetiv, *The Persian Gulf Crisis*, 65.
42. Mazarr, Snider, and Blackwell, Jr., *Desert Storm*, 53–4.
43. Freedman and Karsh, *The Gulf Conflict*, 217.
44. Ibid., 218.
45. Mazarr, Snider, and Blackwell, Jr., *Desert Storm*, 55.
46. Khadduri and Ghareeb, *War in the Gulf*, 148.
47. Quoted in Freedman and Karsh, *The Gulf Conflict*, 223.
48. Spitzer, "The Conflict Between Congress and the President Over War," 28.
49. Ibid., 25–6.
50. Ibid., 29.
51. Mazarr, Snider, and Blackwell, Jr., *Desert Storm*, 59.
52. Yetiv, *The Persian Gulf Crisis*, 17. Secretary of State Baker agreed that the announcement was handled poorly. The president, however, did consult King Fahd of Saudi Arabia. See Baker, "The Gulf War: An Oral History."

53. Freedman and Karsh, *The Gulf Conflict*, 224.
54. Quoted in Spitzer, "The Conflict Between Congress and the President Over War," 29.
55. Mazarr, Snider, and Blackwell, Jr., *Desert Storm*, 65.
56. Freedman and Karsh, *The Gulf Conflict*, 199–233.
57. Mazarr, Snider, and Blackwell, Jr., *Desert Storm*, 67.
58. See Freedman and Karsh, *The Gulf Conflict*, 234.
59. Quoted in Mazarr, Snider, and Blackwell, Jr., *Desert Storm*, 71–3.
60. The only two advisers Bush consulted were Cheney and Scowcroft. However, the national security adviser still feared that a willingness to negotiate with Iraq could signal that the Bush administration lacked resolve. See Freedman and Karsh, *The Gulf Conflict*, 235–6.
61. See Mazarr, Snider, and Blackwell, Jr., *Desert Storm*, 74.
62. Freedman and Karsh, *The Gulf Conflict*, 241.
63. Quoted in ibid., 236.
64. Yetiv, *The Persian Gulf Crisis*, 26–7.
65. Quoted in Mazarr, Snider, and Blackwell, Jr., *Desert Storm*, 74, 80, and 84–6; and Spitzer, "The Conflict Between Congress and the President Over War," 33.
66. Yetiv, *The Persian Gulf Crisis*, 21; see also Spitzer, "The Conflict Between Congress and the President Over War," 34.
67. Quoted in Yetiv, *The Persian Gulf Crisis*, 67.
68. Quoted in Wayne, "President Bush Goes to War," 38.
69. Mazarr, Snider, and Blackwell, Jr., *Desert Storm*, 77.
70. Woodward, *The Commanders*, 350.
71. Powell, "The Gulf War: An Oral History." The air campaign had been going on since mid-January 1991.
72. Ibid. The words "psychologically unprepared" are Bush and Scowcroft's own words. See also George Bush and Brent Scowcroft, "Why We Didn't Go to Baghdad," in *The Iraq War Reader*, ed. Sifry and Cerf, 101.
73. The air campaign had been going on since January 16, 1991.
74. See Steven R. Weisman, "Pre-Emption Evolves From an Idea to Official Action," *The New York Times*, March 22, 2004.
75. Dolan, "Foreign Policy on the Offensive," 10. As explained by John Lewis Gaddis, prior to September 11, U.S. foreign policy-makers differentiated between preemption and prevention. "Preemption" meant taking military action against a state that was about to launch an attack. "Prevention" meant starting a war against a state that might, at some future point, pose such risks. In mounting its post–September 11 offensive, the Bush administration conflated these terms, using the word preemption to justify what turned out to be a "preventive" action against Saddam Hussein's Iraq. See John Lewis Gaddis, "Grand Strategy in the Second Term," *Foreign Affairs*, vol. 84, no. 1, (January/February 2005), 4.
76. The letter appears in *The Iraq War Reader*, ed. Sifry and Cerf, 199–201.

77. See Weisman, "Pre-Emption Evolves From an Idea to Official Action."
78. Speech by President Bill Clinton, "The Costs of Action Must be Weighed Against the Price of Inaction. Excerpts of the speech appear in *The Iraq War Reader*, ed. Sifry and Cerf, 205–9.
79. Condoleezza Rice, "Promoting the National Interest," *Foreign Affairs*, vol. 79, no. 1 (January/February 2000): 53 and 60.
80. Condoleezza Rice, "Why We Know Iraq is Lying," in *The Iraq War Reader*, ed. Sifry and Cerf, 452.
81. Woodward, *Plan of Attack*, 119–20.
82. Quoted in Robert Novak, "No Meeting in Prague," in *The Iraq War Reader*, ed. Sifry and Cerf, 266.
83. Woodward, *Plan of Attack*, 164.
84. Quoted in Clarke, *Against All Enemies*, 231.
85. *The 9/11 Commission Report*, 335–6.
86. Ibid., 334. According to the Commission's Report, Bush did not concur with Clarke that he had ordered him to ascertain whether there was a link, but he does acknowledge that he might have asked him at some other time about Iraq and al Qaeda. See also Clarke, *Against All Enemies*, 32.
87. Walter Pincus and Dana Milbank, "Al Qaeda-Hussein Link Dismissed," *The Washington Post*, June 17, 2004.
88. Quoted in ibid.
89. Presentation by Secretary of State Colin Powell to the UN Security Council, "A Threat to International Peace and Security," February 6, 2003. Excerpts of the presentation appear in *The Iraq War Reader*, ed. Sifry and Cerf, 475 and 477. Not every member in the Bush administration cared whether there was a connection between Hussein and al Qaeda. Rumsfeld, for instance, noted in early May 2002 that in his mind it did not really matter whether there was a link between al Qaeda and Saddam Hussein to "justify U.S. military action against Iraq to remove Saddam from power." As already explained, for him the real cause was the development of weapons of mass destruction by the Baghdad regime.
90. Quoted in Hybel, *Made by the U.S.A.*, 237–8.
91. Rice, "Promoting the National Interest," 49–50.
92. Woodward, *Bush At War*, 131.
93. Woodward, *Plan of Attack*, 86–9.
94. Quoted in ibid., 154–5.
95. Quoted in Michael T. Klare, "Deciphering the Bush Administration's Motives," in *The Gulf War Reader*, ed. Sifry and Cerf, 399.
96. Given the United States's long-standing dependence on Persian Gulf oil, it will not be necessary to conduct a similar analysis of the fourth rationale.
97. See David Barstow, William J. Broad, and Jeff Gerth, "How the White House Embraced Disputed Arms Intelligence," *The New York Times*, October 4, 2004.

98. A centrifuge is a device that rotates rapidly and uses centrifugal force to separate substances of different densities.
99. See Barstow, Broad, and Gerth, "How the White House Embraced Disputed Arms."
100. Quoted in ibid.
101. Ibid.
102. Ibid.
103. Ibid.
104. A review of the National Intelligence Estimate by the Senate Select Committee on Intelligence concluded that the report may very well be one of the most flawed documents in the history of American intelligence. For a review of the Senate's report, see ibid. and Thomas Power, "How Bush Got It Wrong," *The New York Review of Books*, vol. 51, no. 14, September 23, 2004.
105. Woodward, *Plan of Attack*, 199.
106. Ibid., 293.
107. Barstow, Broad, and Gerth, "How the White House Embraced Disputed Arms Intelligence."
108. Wolfowitz voiced his comments just prior to Bush's 2003 State of the Union address. See James Risen, David E. Sanger, and Thom Shanker, "In Sketchy Data, Trying to Gauge Iraq Threat," *The New York Times*, July 19, 2003.
109. Ibid.
110. Commission on the Intelligence Capabilities of the Unites States Regarding Weapons of Mass Destruction, *Report to the President*, March 31, 2005. Available from http://www.wmd.gov/report/report.html.
111. Quoted in Clarke, *Against All Enemies*, 231.
112. Ibid., 33.
113. *The 9/11 Commission Report*, 335–6.
114. Clarke, *Against All Enemies*, 231.
115. The prisoner, Ibn al-Shaykh al-Libi, withdrew his claims about ties between Iraq and al Qaeda in January 2004. See Douglas Jehl, "Qaeda–Iraq Link U.S. Cited Is Tied to Coercion Claim," *The New York Times*, December 9, 2005.
116. From the Office of Carl Levin, United States Senator, "Levin Releases Newly Declassified Intelligence Documents on Iraq-al Qaeda Relationship." (Washington, DC: April 15, 2005).
117. Brent Scowcroft, "Don't Attack Saddam," in *The Iraq War Reader*, ed. Sifry and Cerf, 295. Originally published in *The Wall Street Journal*, August 15, 2002.
118. Woodward, *Plan of Attack*, 206.
119. Quoted in Pincus and Milbank, "Al Qaeda–Hussein." See also Woodward, *Plan of Attack*, 300; and William O. Beeman,

"Al Qaeda-Iraq Connection Tenuous at Best," *Pacific News Service*, February 6, 2003.
120. See *The 9/11 Commission Report*, 61.
121. Ibid., 468, footnote 55.
122. It was Cheney who said in late 2001 that it was "pretty well confirmed" that Mohamed Atta had met with a senior Iraqi intelligence official before the attacks, in April 2000, in Prague, but subsequently said that it was not possible to prove or disprove whether the meeting took place. See Pincus and Milbank, "Al Qaeda-Hussein Link."
123. See *The 9/11 Commission Report*, 66.
124. Paul R. Pillar, "Intelligence, Policy, and the War in Iraq," *Foreign Affairs* (March/April 2006). Available from http://www.foreignaffairs.org/20060301faessay85202/paul-r-pillar/intelligence-policy-and-t . . ., accessed May 7, 2006.
125. See Robert Dahl, *Polyarchy: Participation and Opposition* (New Haven: Yale University Press, 1971), 3–20; and Larry Diamond, Jonathan Hartlyn, Juan J. Linz, and Seymour Martin Lipset, eds., *Democracy in Developing Countries: Latin America* (Boulder, CO: Lynne Rienner Publisher, 1999), ix.
126. See Stein Rokkan, "Formation and Nation-Building: A Possible Paradigm for Research on Variations Within Europe," in *The Formation of National States in Western Europe*, ed. Charles Tilly (Princeton: Princeton University Press, 1975), 571–2.
127. Larry Diamond, Jonathan Hartlyn and Juan J. Linz, "Introduction: Politics, Society, and Democracy in Latin America," in *Democracy in Developing Countries: Latin America*, ed. Diamond, Hartlyn, Linz, and Lipset.
128. See Juan J. Linz and Alfred Stepan, *Problems of Democratic Transition and Consolidation: Southern Europe, South America and Post-Communist Europe* (Baltimore: Johns Hopkins University Press, 1997), Ch. 2.
129. For a discussion of the differences between harmony, cooperation and discord, see Robert Keohane, *After Hegemony* (Princeton: Princeton University Press, 1984), 51–7.
130. See Rokkan, "Formation and Nation-Building," 586–8. As Rokkan notes, the closer the ties of interaction between urban and rural economic elites within a particular territory, the greater the chances for territorial centralizers to consolidate the power of the state.
131. Diamond, Hartlyn, and Linz, "Democracy in Latin America," 34 and 54.
132. Abraham Lowenthal, "The United States and Latin American Democracy: Learning from History," in *Exporting Democracy—The United States and Latin America: Case Studies*, ed. Abraham Lowenthal (Baltimore: Johns Hopkins University Press, 1991), 271.

133. These are some of the main conclusions Abraham Lowenthal derived from the analyses of seven Latin American cases conducted by eight scholars. See ibid., 278.
134. See Laurence Whitehead, "The Imposition of Democracy," in *Exporting Democracy—The United States and Latin America: Case Studies*, ed. Abraham Lowenthal (Baltimore: Johns Hopkins University Press, 1991), 234.
135. See David Fromkin, *A Peace to End All Peace* (New York: Henry Hold and Company, 1989), 450 and 503.
136. See David Rieff, "The Shiite Surge," *The New York Times Magazine*, February 1, 2004.
137. See Dilip Hiro, "The Post-Saddam Problem," in *The Iraq War Reader*, ed. Sifry and Cerf, 560–3. Hiro first published his assessment of the differences between Japan and Iraq in *The Nation* on January 6, 2003, more than two months before the Bush administration ordered the invasion of Iraq. Jeffrey Record arrives at a similar conclusion in *Dark Victory: America's Second War against Iraq* (Annapolis, MD: Naval Institute Press, 2994), 86–8. Moreover, James Webb, a former secretary of the navy, warned the Bush administration in September 2002 not to compare Iraq with Japan. See James Webb, "Heading for Trouble," *The Washington Post*, September 4, 2002.
138. Hiro, "The Post-Saddam Problem," 560–3.
139. See William R. Keylor, *The Twentieth Century World* (New York: Oxford University Press, 1996), 252.
140. For nearly two years, each of the three invading countries ruled a separate region. The Soviet Union ruled the fourth one.
141. Anonymous, *Imperial Hubris*, 182. CIA Director Porter J. Gross acknowledged this much to members of the Senate Select Committee on Intelligence nearly two years after the United States had launched its attack on Iraq. "Islamic extremists," stated Gross, "are exploiting the Iraqi conflict to recruit new anti-U.S. jihadists." He also noted that the "Iraq conflict, while not a cause for extremism, has become a cause for extremists." Vice Admiral Lowell E. Jacoby, the director of the DIA, backed Gross's analysis. Iraq insurgency, he stated, has grown "in size and complexity over the past year." Quoted in Dana Priest and Josh White, "War Helps Recruit Terrorists, Hill Told," in *The Washington Post*, February 17, 2005.
142. Key sections of the report appear in Michael R. Gordon and General Bernard E. Trainor, *Cobra II* (New York: Pantheon Books, 2006), 570–1.
143. See Conrad C. Crane and W. Andrew Terrill, *Reconstructing Iraq: Insights, Challenges, and Missions for Military Forces in a Post-Conflict Scenario* (Carlisla, PA: U. S. Army War College, February 2003).
144. Quoted by Mark Danner in his op-ed, "A Doctrine Left Behind," *The New York Times*, November 21, 2004.

145. Woodward, *Plan of Attack*, 150.
146. Ibid., 206.
147. Richard Haass, "Truth, War and Consequences: Interviews," *PBS Frontline*. Available from http://www.pbs.org/wgbh/pages/frontline/shows/truth/ interviews/haas.html, accessed February 20, 2005.
148. Quoted in Anonymous, *Imperial Hubris*, 15.
149. Nicholas Lemann, "The War on What?" in *The Iraq War Reader*, ed. Sifry and Cerf, 292–3.
150. Pat Buchanan, "The War Party's Imperial Plans," in *The Iraq War Reader*, ed. Sifry and Cerf, 308.
151. Michael R. Gordon, " 'Catastrophic Success: The Strategy to Secure Iraq Did Not Foresee a 2nd War," *The New York Times*, October 19, 2004.
152. Ibid.
153. Robert Kagan and William Kristol, "What To Do About Iraq," in *The Gulf War Reader*, ed. Micah L. Sifry and Christopher Cerf (New York: Random House, 1991), 245.
154. Quoted in Gordon and Trainor, *Cobra II*, 100.
155. Quoted in Record, *Dark Victory*, 86.

Chapter Five   The Apple Sometimes Falls Close to the Tree

1. For a more detailed discussion of the various techniques, see Pfiffner, "Presidential Policy-Making and the Gulf War", 7–9.
2. Ibid., 7. See also Alexander L. George, "The Case of Multiple Advocacy in Making Foreign Policy," *American Political Science Review* 66 (September, 1972): 751–85.
3. Pfiffner, "Presidential Policy-Making and the Gulf War," 8.
4. Woodward, *The Commanders*, 74.
5. See Renshon, "Good Judgment," 87 and 92.
6. Colin Powell, "The Gulf War: An Oral History." The power game that often ensues between the advisers is explained by Jean A. Garrison, who writes: "The advisor[s] occupying the best structural position ha[ve] an advantage in the advisory process . . . The narrowing of access enables them to control the presentation of options to the president." Garrison adds: "[T]he tactics used depend upon the status and authority of both the influencer and the target of influence. Scowcroft and Cheney, whose rankings were higher than Powell's, used them to restrict the general's access to President Bush." See Garrison, *Games Advisors Play*, 139.
7. One of the great fears on the part of the Saudi leadership was that the deployment of U.S. forces would embolden Islamic fundamentalists to criticize and initiate aggressive actions against the government for

allowing infidels to enter a land that Muslims considered sacred. Ultimately this fear proved to be justified.
8. Yetiv, *The Persian Gulf Crisis*, 63 and footnote 14 on page 80.
9. Woodward, *The Commanders*, 320.
10. For an expanded discussion of theories that deal with the ways foreign policy-makers use historical analogies, please refer to chapter 1.
11. Yetiv, *The Persian Gulf Crisis*, 63.
12. Quoted in Wayne, "President Bush Goes to War," 40.
13. Renshon, "Good Judgment, and the Lack Thereof, in the Gulf War," 86; see also Wayne, "President Bush Goes to War," 36.
14. Renshon, "Good Judgment, and the Lack Thereof, in the Gulf War," 91.
15. Quoted in Wayne, "President Bush Goes to War," 36.
16. Ibid., 40. In October 1990, Bush's chief pollster Robert Teeter informed the president "the Hitler analogy had not rung true because 'in the eyes of a majority of people, there couldn't be somebody more harmful than Hitler.'" See Freedman and Karsh, *The Gulf Conflict*, 222.
17. Quoted in Yetiv, *The Persian Gulf Crisis*, 68.
18. Quoted in Woodward, *The Commanders*, 277.
19. See Hybel, *Power Over Rationality*, 66.
20. Quoted in Wayne, "President Bush Goes to War," 39 and 40.
21. Baker, "The Gulf War: An Oral History."
22. Richard Cheney, "The Gulf War: An Oral History," *PBS Frontline*. Available from http://www/pbs.org/wgbh/pages/frontline/gulf/oral/cheney/1.html, accessed February 23, 2003.
23. Haass, "The Gulf War: An Oral History."
24. See Hybel, *Power Over Rationality*, 21–2. For a thorough elaboration of schema theory, see Larson, *Origins of Containment*, 50–7.
25. Powell, "The Gulf War: An Oral History."
26. Quoted in Hybel, *Power Over Rationality*, 76.
27. Powell, "The Gulf War: An Oral History."
28. Quoted in Hybel, *Power Over Rationality*, 77.
29. Quoted in Yetiv, *The Persian Gulf Crisis*, 69.
30. Baker, "The Gulf War: An Oral History."
31. Quoted in Hybel, *Power Over Rationality*, 77.
32. Powell, "The Gulf War: An Oral History."
33. Quoted in Andrew Cockburn and Patrick Cockburn, "We Have Saddam Hussein Still Here," in *The Iraq War Reader*, ed. Micah L. Sifry and Christopher Cerf (New York: Simon and Schuster, 2004), 93.
34. Baker, "The Gulf War: An Oral History."
35. Powell, "The Gulf War: An Oral History."
36. Cheney, "The Gulf War: An Oral History."
37. Khadduri and Ghareeb, *War in the Gulf*, 175.
38. The long quote is a compilation of two answers to two separate questions. In both instances, however, Cheney referred to the challenges the

United States would have faced had the Bush administration decided to march toward Baghdad with the intent of overthrowing the Saddam regime. See Cheney, "The Gulf War: An Oral History."
39. Bush and Scowcroft, "Why We Didn't Go To Baghdad," 101–2 in *The Iraq War Reader*, ed. Sifry and Cerf.
40. Baker, "The Gulf War: An Oral History."
41. Bush and Scowcroft, "Why We Didn't Go To Baghdad," 102.
42. Khadduri and Ghareeb, *War in the Gulf*, 178.
43. Ibid.
44. Scowcroft, "The Gulf War: An Oral History."
45. Baker, "The Gulf War: An Oral History." The military, in particular, was ill-at-ease with the idea of continuing the war after the president's main goal had been attained. See Freedman and Karsh, *The Gulf Conflict*, 405.
46. Statement by Richard Haass. Quoted in Freedman and Karsh, *The Gulf Conflict*, 405.
47. The quote is a compilation of responses to two different questions. The assemblage does not distort Scowcroft's overall answer. Scowcroft, "The Gulf War: An Oral History."
48. Haass, "The Gulf War: An Oral History."
49. Cheney, "The Gulf War: An Oral History."
50. Quoted in Freedman and Karsh, *The Gulf Conflict*, 417.
51. Quoted in Cockburn and Cockburn, "We Have Saddam Still Here," 96.
52. The United States did invade the southern part of Iraq for a brief period.
53. Woodward, *Plan of Attack*, 9–12.
54. Ibid., 19–20.
55. See Jervis, *Perception and Misperception in International Relations*, 220.
56. See Larson, *Origins of Containment*, 53.
57. Quoted in Peter J. Boyer, "The Believer," *The New Yorker*, November 1, 2004.
58. Kenneth Pollack, "Can We Really Deter a Nuclear-Armed Saddam?" in *The Iraq War Reader*, ed. Sifry and Cerf, 403.
59. James Risen, David E. Sanger, and Thom Shanker, "In Sketchy Data, Trying to Gauge Iraq Threat," *The New York Times*, July 19, 2003.
60. Ibid.
61. Sarah Graham-Brown and Chris Toensing, "A Backgrounder on Inspections and Sanctions," in *The Iraq War Reader*, ed. Sifry and Cerf, 165–6.
62. However, analysts at the Department of State, argued that "the activities we have detected do not . . . add up to a compelling case" that Iraq was pursuing "an integrated and comprehensive approach to acquire nuclear weapons." See Risen, Sanger, and Shanker, "In Sketchy Data, Trying to Gauge Iraq Threat."

63. The words are Woodward's own. See Woodward, *Plan of Attack*, 290.
64. Ibid., 21–2. For an analysis of the internal debate that ensued regarding Iraq during the early months of the second Bush administration, see Dolan, "Foreign Policy on the Offensive," 3–22.
65. Quoted in Woodward, *Bush at War*, 84.
66. Ibid., 84–5.
67. Woodward, *Plan of Attack*, 26.
68. Quoted in Steven R. Weisman, "Pre-emption Evolves From an Idea to Official Action," *The New York Times*, March 23, 2004.
69. Quoted in Woodward, *Plan of Attack*, 25.
70. Woodward, *Bush at War*, 37.
71. Quoted in Woodward, *Plan of Attack*, 27.
72. Nicholas Lemann, "The Next World Order," in *The Iraq War Reader*, ed. Sifry and Cerf, 256.
73. Risen, Sanger, and Shanker, "In Sketchy Data, trying to Gauge Iraq Threat."
74. James D. Barber, *The Presidential Character: Predicting Performance in the White House* (Englewoods Cliffs, NJ: Prentice-Hall, 1985).
75. Cheney corroborated this point. During a private gathering with friends at his home, the vice president noted that democracy "in the Middle East . . . [is] what's driving him [the president]." See Woodward, *Plan of Attack*, 412.
76. Bush's attitude toward how he would be perceived long after he left the presidency changed significantly just after a couple of years. As time went by and the war proved to be markedly more costly and cumbersome than he had originally assumed, his concern about the way history would judge his decision to overthrow Saddam Hussein's regime intensified.
77. Woodward, *Plan of Attack*, 443.
78. Woodward, *Bush at War*, 32.
79. Woodward, *Plan of Attack*, 86–9.
80. Quoted in Ron Suskind, "Without a Doubt," *The New York Times Magazine*, October 17, 2004, 41.
81. The statement that Bush lacked "curiosity about complex issues" comes from Carl Levin, the Democratic senator from Michigan. Levin's comment should not be construed as the criticism from an opposing politician. Many members of the Republican Party voiced similar impressions about the president's disinterest in deciphering the possible complexities of a problem. We will address this matter shortly. See ibid., 47. The argument that Bush's leadership bordered on the hurried and that he is a president who wants action and solutions is Woodward's. See Woodward, *Bush at War*, 255–6.
82. See Woodward, *Plan of Attack*, 53–66.

83. Eric Schmitt and Joel Brinkley, "State Department Study Foresaw Trouble Now Plaguing Iraq," *The New York Times*, October 18, 2003.
84. Zalmay Khalilzad, Special Assistant to the President for Near East, South West Asian, and North African Affairs, "The Future of Iraq Policy." Remarks at *The Washington Institute's 2002 Weinberg Founders Conference*, October 5, 2002.
85. Bob Woodward, "Decision Iraq—Would John Kerry Have Done Things Differently?" *The Washington Post*, October 24, 2004.
86. Richard Haass, "Truth, War and Consequences: What Went Wrong? Turf Wars and the Future of Iraq: Interview."
87. Richard Perle, Richard Haass, Kanan Mikaya, and Laith Kubba, "Truth, War and Consequences: What Went Wrong? Turf Wars and the Future of Iraq." Available from http://www.pbs.org/wgbh/pages/frontline/shows/truth/fighting/trufwars.html, accessed December 30, 2004.
88. Woodward, *Plan of Attack*, 280–4.
89. Ibid., 328.
90. Schmitt and Brinkley, "State Department Study Foresaw Trouble Now Plaguing Iraq."
91. Ibid. See also Robert Dreyfuss, "Humpty Dumpty in Baghdad," *The American Prospect*, 14, Issue 5 (May 1, 2003).
92. Major Isaiah Wilson III served as an official historian of the war campaign and as a war planner in Iraq. Wilson presented his project to Cornell University. See Thomas E. Ricks, "Army Historian Cites Lack of Postwar Plan," *The Washington Post*, December 25, 2004.
93. See Crane and Terrill, *Reconstructing Iraq*. The authors acknowledge that the staff of Gen. Douglas MacArthur developed Operation BLACKLIST—plan for Japan's occupation—in just over three months, but then add "analysis for such a course had been going on for years back in the United States."
94. Gordon, "Catastrophic Success."
95. Quoted in *Newsweek*, "Iraq: Imagining the Day After," February 12, 2003.
96. Woodward, *Plan of Attack*, 152.
97. Douglas Jehl and David E. Sanger, "Prewar Assessment on Iraq Saw Chance of Strong Divisions," *The New York Times*, September 28, 2004.
98. As quoted by Gordon in " 'Catastrophic Success': The Strategy to Secure Iraq Did Not Foresee a 2nd War."
99. Ibid.
100. Dick Cheney, "The Risks of Inaction are Far Greater Than the Risk of Action," in *The Iraq War Reader*, ed. Sifry and Cerf, 299.
101. Woodward, *Plan of Attack*, 162.

102. Woodward, *Plan of Attack*, 152.
103. Ibid., 261–2.
104. Quoted in Record, *Dark Victory*, 86.
105. Gordon, "Catastrophic Success."
106. See Larry Diamond, "What Went Wrong in Iraq," *Foreign Affairs* (Sep./Oct. 2004).
107. Gordon, "Catastrophic Success." For discussions of the mistakes made by the United States as it sought to restructure Iraq, see Michael O'Hanlon, "Iraq Without a Plan," *Policy Review*, no. 128 (December 2004–January 2005); and Diamond, "What Went Wrong in Iraq."
108. Robert F. Kennedy, *Thirteen Days: A Memoir of the Cuban Missile Crisis* (New York: W. W. Norton and Company, 1971), 11.
109. To contend that since the Kuwait war almost everyone in the United States had loathed the Saddam Hussein regime is an understatement. But not everyone outside the Bush administration assumed that the Iraqi leader was markedly worse, more out of control, and more violent than other world leaders. Those who posited this interpretation, moreover, asserted that Saddam Hussein's behavior showed he could be contained and deterred. Some did acknowledge that containment and deterrence were not risk-free, but emphasized that it was less hazardous than beginning a conflict that could hasten the danger they were designed to avert. Moreover, not everyone outside the Bush administration who viewed Saddam Hussein as an untrustworthy, aggressive, and risk-driven leader and believed that he could not be deterred, was convinced that a preventive war was the best solution. The threat of war, according to some of them, might compel the Iraqi leader to permit weapons inspections to reenter Iraq, and this in turn could lead to the uncovering and elimination of WMD stockpiles and production facilities. See John Mearsheimer and Stephen Walt, "An Unnecessary War," in *The Iraq War Reader*, ed. Sifry and Cerf, 414–15; and Richard K. Betts, "Suicide From Fear of Death?" in *The Iraq War Reader*, ed. Sifry and Cerf, 430.
110. Quoted in Woodward, *Plan of Attack*, 27.
111. See ibid., 98 and 108–9.
112. Ibid., 152–3. As Bush acknowledged, his administration did not think about developing a diplomatic strategy until August 2002.
113. Ibid., 150–1. See also Maura Reynolds, "Books Depict Bush as Instinct-Driven Leader," in *Los Angeles Times*, May 3, 2004.
114. Woodward, *Plan of Attack*, 176 and 184.
115. Ibid., 51.
116. Ibid., 115.
117. *Haass*, "Truth, War and Consequences: Interviews."
118. David Manning, "The Secret Downing Street Memo," *The Sunday Times*, May 1, 2005.
119. Woodward, *Plan of Attack*, 169.

120. Quoted in ibid., 206.
121. Ibid., 234.
122. Ibid., 234, 251–2, and 293. According to a commission set up by President Bush and led by former senator Charles S. Robb and appellate court judge Laurence H. Silberman, the work of the UN weapons inspectors was routinely dismissed by the White House. See Dafna Linzer, "Panel: U.S. Ignored Work of U.N. Arms Inspectors," *The Washington Post*, April 3, 2005.
123. See Irving L. Janis and Leon Mann, *Decisionmaking: Psychological Analyses of Conflict, Choice, and Commitment* (New York: Free Press, 1977).
124. Hybel, *Power Over Rationality*, 27.
125. Quoted in Walter Williams, "Bush's decision defined by ideology," *Seattle Post-Intelligencer*, (September 28, 2004).
126. Quoted in Woodward, *Plan of Attack*, 151.
127. Woodward, *Bush at War*, 255.
128. Suskind, "Without a Doubt," 49.
129. Suskind, *The Price of Loyalty*, 325–8.
130. Quoted in ibid., 171.
131. In his attempt to summarize the extent to which Bush comprehended the implications of his decision, Woodward writes, "as I listened [to Bush] I glimpsed what Powell had apparently seen—uncertainty that the president fully grasped the potential consequences of war." See Woodward, *Plan of Attack*, 79–80, and 152.
132. Quoted in Christopher Marquis, "How Powerful Can 16 Words Be?" *The New York Times*, July 20, 2003.
133. Manning, "The Secret Downing Street Memo."
134. See Woodward, *Bush at War*, 257–8.
135. Suskind, "Without a Doubt," 47.
136. Woodward, *Plan of Attack*, 152.
137. Suskind, *The Price of Loyalty*, 117.
138. Woodward, *Bush at War*, 259.
139. Quoted in Woodward, *Plan of Attack*, 271.
140. Commission on the Intelligence Capabilities, *Report to the President*.

Chapter Six   The Absence of a Rational Process

1. See G. John Ikenberry ed., *American Foreign Policy*, Fourth Edition (New York: Longman, 2002), 3–5.
2. This is not to suggest that Powell failed to present containment as a viable policy. He did present it and noted that it was a policy that had merit. He never stated, however, that it was a better choice than going to war. See Woodward, *The Commanders*, 301.
3. Theodore Sorensen, *Decision-Making in the White House* (New York: Columbia University Press, 1963), 90.

4. Janis, *Victims of Groupthink*.
5. Pillar, "Intelligence, Policy, and the War in Iraq."
6. There is an important distinction between using history intelligently and being a prisoner of history. An intelligent user of history will always ask: To what extent does this case resemble an earlier one? He will also inquire whether the previous case that he is focusing on replicates itself in other instances. Any decision-maker who fails or refuses to pose these two simple questions risks becoming a captive of history and deriving the wrong set of inferences.
7. See Jervis, *Perception and Misperception*, 220.
8. Quoted in Robert Kennedy, *Thirteen Days: A Memoir of the Cuban Missile Crisis* (New York: W.W. Norton and Company, 1971), 11.
9. John F. Burns and Eric Schmitt, "Outlook bleak for Iraqi war," *New York Times News Service* printed by *The Day*, May 19, 2005.
10. George Orwell, "Politics and the English Language." In *George Orwell: Selected Essays* (Harmondsworth: Penguin, 1957), 157. Reason and rationality are not synonyms, but rationality without reason is not possible.
11. See Jon Elster, *Strong Feeling—Emotion, Addiction, and Human Behavior* (Cambridge: The MIT Press, 2000).

BIBLIOGRAPHY

Achen, Christopher, and Duncan Snidal. "Rational Deterrence Theory and Comparative Case Studies." *World Politics* 41, no. 2 (January 1989).

Anonymous. *Imperial Hubris*. Washington, DC: Brassey's, 2004.

Baker, James. "The Gulf War: An Oral History." *PBS: Frontline*. http://www.pbs. org/wgbh/pages/frontline/gulf/oral/baker/1.html.

Barber, James D. *The Presidential Character: Predicting Performance in the White House*. Englewoods Cliffs, NJ: Prentice-Hall, 1985.

Barstow, David, William J. Board, and Jeff Gerth. "How the White House Embraced Disputed Arms Intelligence." *The New York Times*, October 4, 2004.

Beeman, William O. "Al Qaeda—Iraq Connection Tenuous at Best." *Pacific News Service*, February 6, 2003.

Betts, Richard K. "Suicide From Fear of Death." In *The Iraq War Reader*, edited by Micah L. Sifry and Christopher Cerf. New York: Simon and Schuster, 2003.

Boyer, Peter. "The Believer." *The New Yorker*, November 1, 2003.

Buchanan, Pat. "The War Party's Imperial Plans." In *The Iraq War Reader*, edited by Micah L. Sifry and Christopher Cerf. New York: Simon and Schuster, 2003.

Bueno de Mesquita, Bruce. "Forecasting Policy Decisions: An Expected Utility Approach to Post-Khomeini Iran." *Political Science and Politics* 17 (1984).

Bueno de Mesquita, Bruce, and David Lalman. "Domestic Opposition and Foreign War." *American Political Science Review* 84 (1990).

Bullock, John, and Harvey Morris. *Saddam's War: The Origins of the Kuwait Conflict and the International Response*. London: Faber and Faber, 1991.

Burke, John P., and Fred I. Greenstein. *How Presidents Test Reality*. New York: Russell Sage Foundation, 1991.

Burns, John F., and Eric Schmitt. "Outlook Bleak for Iraqi War." *The New York Times News Service* printed by *The Day*, May 19, 2005.

Bush, George, and Brent Scowcroft. "Why We Didn't Go to Baghdad." In *The Iraq War Reader*, edited by Micah L. Sifry and Christopher Cerf. New York: Simon and Schuster, 2003.

———. *A World Transformed*. New York: Alfred Knopf, 1998.

Cannon, Lou. *President Reagan. The Role of a Lifetime.* New York: Simon and Schuster, 1991.

Cheney, Dick. "The Risks Of Inaction Are Far Greater Than The Risk of Action." In *The Iraq War Reader,* edited by Micah L. Sifry and Christopher Cerf. New York: Simon and Schuster, 2003.

Cheney, Richard. "The Gulf War: An Oral History." *PBS: Frontline.* http://www.pbs.org/ wgbh/pages/frontline/gulf/oral/cheney/1.html.

Clarke, Richard A. *Against All Enemies: Inside America's War on Terror.* New York: Simon and Schuster, 2004.

———. *Memorandum for Condoleezza Rice: Presidential Policy Initiative/Review—The Al-Qida Network.* Washington, DC: National Security Council, January 25, 2001.

Clausewitz, Carl von. "On the Nature of War." In *Classics of International Relations,* edited by John Vasquez. Englewood Cliffs, NJ: Prentice-Hall, 1990.

Clinton, Bill. "The Costs of Action Must be Weighed Against the Price of Inaction." In *The Iraq War Reader,* edited by Micah L. Sifry and Christopher Cerf. New York: Simon and Schuster, 2003.

Cockburn, Andrew, and Patrick Cockburn. "We Have Saddam Hussein Still Here." In *The Iraq War Reader,* edited by Micah L. Sifry and Christopher Cerf. New York: Simon and Schuster, 2003.

Commission on the Intelligence Capabilities of the Unites States Regarding Weapons of Mass Destruction. *Report to the President, March 31, 2005.* http://www.wmd.gov/report/report/html.

Crane, Conrad C., and W. Andrew Terrill. *Reconstructing Iraq: Insights, Challenges, and Missions for Military Forces in a Post-Conflict Scenario.* Carlisla, PA: U.S. Army War College, February 2003.

Dahl, Robert. *Polyarchy: Participation and Opposition.* New Haven: Yale University Press, 1971.

Danner, Mark. "A Doctrine Left Behind." *The New York Times,* November 21, 2004.

Diamond, Larry. "What Went Wrong in Iraq." *Foreign Affairs* 83, no. 5 (September/October 2004).

Diamond, Larry, Jonathan Hartlyn, and Juan Linz. "Introduction: Politics, Society, and Democracy in Latin America." In *Democracy in Developing Countries: Latin America,* edited by Larry Diamond, Jonathan Hartlyn, Juan Linz, and Seymour Martin Lipset. Boulder, CO: Lynne Reinner Publisher, 1999.

Diamond, Larry, Jonathan Hartlyn, Juan Linz, and Seymour Martin Lipset, eds. *Democracy in Developing Countries: Latin America.* Boulder, CO: Lynne Reinner Publisher, 1999.

Dolan, Chris J. "Foreign Policy on the Offensive." In *Striking First. The Preventive War Doctrine and the Reshaping of U.S. Foreign Policy,* edited by Betty Glad and Chris J. Dolan. New York: Palgrave Macmillan, 2004.

Dreyfuss, Robert. "Humpty Dumpty in Baghdad." *The American Prospect* 14, Issue 5 (May 1, 2003).

Elliot, Michael. "Could 9/11 Have Been Prevented?" *Time*, August 4, 2002.

Elster, Jon. *Strong Feeling, Emotion, Addiction, and Human Behavior.* Cambridge: The MIT Press, 2000.

"Fatawa Urging Jihad Against Americans." *Al—Quds a'l-'Arab* (in Arabic), February 23, 1998.

Fernandez, Raquel, and Doni Rodrik. "Resistance to Reform: Status Quo Bias in the Presence of Individual Specific Uncertainty." *American Economic Review* 81 (December 1991).

Freedman, Lawrence, and Ephraim Karsh. *The Gulf Conflict, 1990–1991.* Princeton: Princeton University Press, 1993.

Fromkin, David. *A Peace to End all Peace.* New York: Henry Hold and Company, 1989.

Gaddis, John Lewis. "Grand Strategy in the Second Term." *Foreign Affairs* 84, no. 1 (January/February 2005).

Garrison, Jean A. *Games Advisors Play. Foreign Policy in the Nixon and Carter Administrations.* College Station, TX: Texas A & M University Press, 1999.

George, Alexander L. *Presidential Decisionmaking in Foreign Policy: The Effective Use of Information and Advice.* Boulder, CO: Westview Press, 1979.

———. "The Case of Multiple Advocacy in Making Foreign Policy." *American Political Science Review* 66 (September 1972).

George, Alexander L., and Richard Smoke. *Deterrence in American Foreign Policy.* New York: Columbia University Press, 1974.

Glad, Betty. "Can Tyrants be Deterred?" In *Striking First. The Preventive War Doctrine and the Reshaping of U.S. Foreign Policy,* edited by Betty Glad and Chris J. Dolan. New York: Palgrave Macmillan, 2004.

Gordon, Michael. "Catastrophic Success: The Strategy To Secure Iraq Did Not Foresee a 2nd War." *The New York Times,* October 19, 2004.

Gordon, Michael, and General Bernard T. Trainor. *Cobra II.* New York: Pantheon Books, 2006.

Graham-Brown, Sarah, and Chris Toensing. "A Backgrounder on Inspections and Sanctions." In *The Iraq War Reader,* edited by Micah L. Sifry and Christopher Cerf. New York: Simon and Schuster, 2003.

Haas, Richard. "The Gulf War: An Oral History." *PBS: Frontline.* http://www.pbs. org/wgbh/pages/frontline/gulf/oral/haas/1.html.

———. "Truth, War and Consequences." *PBS: Frontline Interview.* http://www.pbs.org/wgbh/pages/frontline/shows/truth/interviews/haas.html.

Halberstam, David. *War in Time of Peace.* New York: Scribner, 2001.

Hartmann, Charles. *Crises in Foreign Policy.* Indianapolis, IN: Bobb-Merrill, 1969.

Hippler, Jochen. "Iraq's Military Power: The German Connection." *Middle East Report* (January–February, 1991).

Hiro, Dilip. "The Post-Saddam Problem." In *The Iraq War Reader*, edited by Micah L. Sifry and Christopher Cerf. New York: Simon and Schuster, 2003.

Hybel, Alex Roberto. *Made by the U.S.A.—The International System*. New York: Palgrave, 2001.

———. *Power Over Rationality: The Bush Administration and the Gulf Crisis*. Albany: State University of New York Press, 1993.

———. *How Leaders Reason: U.S. Intervention in the Caribbean Basin and Latin America*. Oxford: Basil Blackwell, 1990.

———. *The Logic of Surprise in International Conflict*. Lexington. MA: Lexington Books, 1986.

Ikenberry, John, ed. *American Foreign Policy*. New York: Longman, 2002.

———. "Iraq: Imagining the Day After." *Newsweek*, February 12, 2003.

Janis, Irving L., and Leon Mann. *Decisionmaking: Psychological Analyses of Conflict, Choice, and Commitment*. New York: Free Press, 1977.

Janis, Irving. *Victims of Groupthink*. Boston: Houghton Mifflin, 1972.

Jehl, Douglas. "Qaeda–Iraq Link U.S. Cited is Tied to Coercion Claim." *The New York Times*, December 9, 2005.

Jehl, Douglas, and David E. Sanger. "Prewar Assessment in Iraq Saw Chances of Strong Divisions." *The New York Times*, September 28, 2004.

Jentleson, Bruce W. *American Foreign Policy*. New York: W. W. Norton, 2004.

Jervis, Robert. *Perception and Misperception in International Relations*. Princeton: Princeton University Press, 1976.

Kagan, Robert, and William Kristol. "What To Do About Iraq." In *The Iraq War Reader*, edited by Micah L. Sifry and Christopher Cerf. New York: Simon and Schuster, 2003.

Kennedy, Robert. *Thirteen Days: A Memoir of the Cuban Missile Crisis*. New York: W. W. Norton and Company, 1971.

Keohane, Robert. *After Hegemony*. Princeton: Princeton University Press, 1984.

Keylor, William R. *The Twentieth Century World*. New York: Oxford University Press, 1996.

Khadduri, Majid, and Edmund Ghareeb. *War in the Gulf, 1990–1991. The Iraq–Kuwait Conflict and Its Implications*. New York: Oxford University Press, 1997.

Khalilzad, Zalmay. "The Future of Iraq Policy." Remarks at *The Washington Institute's 2002 Weinberg Founders Conference*, October 5, 2002.

Klare, Michael T. "Deciphering the Bush Administration's Motives." In *The Iraq War Reader*, edited by Micah L. Sifry and Christopher Cerf. New York: Simon and Schuster, 2003.

Knorr, Klaus. "Failures in National Intelligence Estimates: The Case of the Cuban Missile Crisis." *World Politics* 16, no. 1 (April 1964).

Krasner, Stephen D. *Defending the National Interest: Raw Materials Investments and U.S. Foreign Policy*. Princeton: Princeton University Press, 1978.

"Kuwait: How the West Blundered." In *The Gulf War Reader*, edited by Micah L. Sifry and Christopher Cerf. Appeared originally in *The Economist*, September 29, 1990. New York: Random House, 1991.

Larson, Deborah Welch. *Origins of Containment*. Princeton: Princeton University Press, 1985.

Lemann, Nicholas. "The Next World Order." In *The Iraq War Reader*, edited by Micah L. Sifry and Christopher Cerf. New York: Simon and Schuster, 2003.

————. "The War on What?" In *The Iraq War Reader*, edited by Micah L. Sifry and Christopher Cerf. New York: Simon and Schuster, 2003.

"Levin Releases Newly Declassified Intelligence Documents on Iraq–al Qaeda Relationship." *Office of U.S. Senator Carl Levin*. Washington, DC: April 15, 2005.

Linz, Juan, and Alfred Stepan. *Problems of Democratic Transition and Consolidation: Southern Europe, South America and Post-Communist Europe*. Baltimore: Johns Hopkins University Press, 1997.

Linzer, Dafna. "Panel: U.S. Ignored Work of U.N. Arms Inspectors." *The Washington Post*, April 3, 2005.

Litchblau, Eric. "9/11 Report Cites Many Warnings About Hijacking." *The New York Times*, February 10, 2005.

Lowenthal, Abraham. "The United States and Latin American Democracy: Learning From History." In *Exporting Democracy—The United States and Latin American Case Studies*, edited by Abraham Lowenthal. Baltimore: Johns Hopkins University Press, 1991.

Macdonald, Scot. *Rolling the Dice. Historical Analogies and Decisions to Use Military Force in Regional Contingencies*. New York: Greenwood Press, 2000.

Manning, David. "The Secret Downing Street Memo." *The Sunday Times*, May 1, 2005.

Marquis, Christopher. "How Powerful Can 16 Words Be?" *The New York Times* July 20, 2003.

May, Ernest. *"Lessons" of the Past. The Use and Misuse of History in American Foreign Policy*. New York: Oxford University Press, 1973.

Mazarr, Michael J., Don M. Snider, and James A. Blackwell, Jr. *Desert Storm—The Gulf War and What We Learned*. Boulder, CO: Westview Press, 1993.

Mearsheimer, John, and Stephen Walt. "An Unnecessary War." In *The Iraq War Reader*, edited by Micah L. Sifry and Christopher Cerf. New York: Simon and Schuster, 2003.

Mintz, Alex. "The Decision to Attack Iraq." *Journal of Conflict Resolutions 37*, no. 4 (December 1993).

Morgenthau, Hans. *Politics Among Nations: The Struggle for Power and Peace*. Revised by Kenneth W. Thompson. New York: Alfred Knopf, 1985.

Neustadt, Richard E., and Ernest May. *Thinking in Time. The Uses of History by Decision Makers*. New York: The Free Press, 1986.

Novak, Robert. "No Meeting in Prague." In *The Iraq War Reader*, edited by Micah L. Sifry and Christopher Cerf. New York: Simon and Schuster, 2003.

O'Hanlon, Michael. "Iraq Without a Plan." *Policy Review*, no. 128 (December 2004–January 2005).

Orwell, George. "Politics and the English Language." In *George Orwell: Selected Essays*. Harmondsworth: Penguin, 1957.

Ostrom Jr., Charles W., and Brian Job. "The President and the Political Use of Force." *American Political Science Review* 80 (1986).

Perle, Richard, Richard Haas, Mikaya Kanan, and Laitha Kubba. "Truth, War and Consequences: What Went Wrong? Turf Wars and the Future of Iraq." *PBS: Frontline*. http://www.pbs.org/wgbh/pages/frontline/shows/truth/fighting/turf wars.html.

Pfiffner, James P. "Presidential Policy-Making and the Gulf War." In *The Presidency and the Persian Gulf War*, edited by Marcia Lynn Whicker, James P. Pfiffner and Raymond A. Moore. Westport, CT: Praeger, 1993.

Pierce, Charles Sanders. "The Fixation of Belief." In *The Essential Pierce*, vol. 1, edited by N. Houser and C. Koesel. Bloomington, IN: Indiana University Press, 1992.

Pillar, Paul R. "Intelligence, Policy, and the War in Iraq." *Foreign Affairs* (March/April 2006). http:www.foreignaffairs.org/20060301faessay85202/ paul-r-pillar/intelligence-policy-and-t . . .

Pincus, Walter, and Dana Milbank. "Al Qaeda–Hussein Link Dismissed." *The Washington Post*, June 17, 2004.

Pollack, Kenneth. "Can We Really Deter a Nuclear-Armed Saddam?" In *The Iraq War Reader*, edited by Micah L. Sifry and Christopher Cerf. New York: Simon and Schuster, 2003.

Powell, Colin. "The Gulf War: An Oral History." *PBS: Frontline*. http://www.pbs. org/wgbh/pages/frontline/gulf/oral/powell/1.html.

———. "Presentation to the U.N. Security Council: A Threat to International Peace and Security." In *The Iraq War Reader*, edited by Micah L. Sifry and Christopher Serf. New York: Simon and Schuster, 2003.

———. *My American Journey*. New York: Random House, 1995.

Power, Thomas. "How Bush Got It Wrong." *The New York Review of Books* 51, no. 14 (September 23, 2004).

Priest, Dana, and Josh White. "War Helps Recruit Terrorists, Hill Told." *The Washington Post*, February 17, 2005.

Record, Jeffrey. *Making History, Thinking History: Munich, Vietnam, and Presidential Uses of Force from Korea to Kosovo*. Annapolis, MD: Naval Institute Press, 2002.

———. *Dark Victory: America's War against Iraq*. Annapolis, MA: Naval Institute Press, 2004.

Renshon, Stanley. "Good Judgment, and the Lack Thereof, in the Gulf War." In *The Political Psychology of the Gulf War*, edited by Stanley Renshon. Pittsburgh: University of Pittsburgh Press, 1993.

Report of the President's Special Review Board (Tower Report). Washington, DC: U.S. Government Printing Office, 1987.

Reynolds, Maura. "Books Depict Bush as Instinct-Driven Leader." *Los Angeles Times*, May 3, 2004.

Rice, Condoleezza. "Why We Know Iraq is Lying." In *The Iraq War Reader*, edited by Micah L. Sifry and Christopher Cerf. New York: Simon and Schuster, 2004.

———. "Promoting the National Interest." *Foreign Affairs* 79, no. 1 (January/ February, 2000).

Ricks, Thomas. "Army Historian Cites Lack of Postwar Plan." *The Washington Post*, December 25, 2004.

Rieff, David. "The Shiite Surge." *The New York Times Magazine*, February 1, 2004.

Risen, James, David E. Sanger, and Thom Shanker. "In Sketchy Data, Trying to Gauge Iraq Threat." *The New York Times*, July 19, 2003.

Rokkan, Stein. "Dimensions of State Formation and Nation-Building: A Possible Paradigm for Research on Variations Within Europe." In *The Formation of National States in Western Europe*, edited by Charles Tilly. Princeton: Princeton University Press, 1975.

Schmitt, Eric, and Joel Brinkley. "State Department Study Foresaw Trouble Now Plaguing Iraq." *The New York Times*, October 18, 2003.

Scowcroft, Brent. "The Gulf War: An Oral History." *PBS: Frontline.*: http://www.pbs.org/wgbh/pages/frontline/gulf/oral/scowcroft/ 1.html.

———. "Don't Attack Saddam." In *The Iraq War Reader*, edited by Micah L. Sifry and Christopher Cerf. New York: Simon and Schuster, 2003.

Shellum, Brian. *A Chronology of Defense Intelligence in the Gulf War: A Research Aid for Analysts*. Washington, DC: DIA History Office, 1997.

Simon, Herbert. *Models of Man*. New York: John Wiley and Sons, 1957.

Sorensen, Theodore. *Decision-Making in the White House*. New York: Columbia University Press, 1963.

Stein, Janice Gross. "Threat-Based Strategies of Conflict Management: Why Did They Fail in the Gulf?" In *The Political Psychology of the Gulf War*, edited by Stanley Renshon. Pittsburgh: University of Pittsburgh, 1993.

———. "Military Deception, Strategic Surprise, and Conventional Discourse: A Political Analysis of Egypt and Israel, 1971–1973." *The Journal of Strategic Studies* 5, no. 1 (March 1982): 92–121.

Stiles, Kendal. *Case Histories in International Politics*. New York: Pearson, 2004.

Suskind, Ron. "Without a Doubt." *The New York Times Magazine*, October 17, 2004.

———. *The Price of Loyalty*. New York: Simon and Schuster, 2004.

"The Glaspie Transcript." In *The Iraq War Reader*, edited by Micah L. Sifry and Christopher Cerf. New York: Simon and Schuster, 2003.

The 9/11 Commission Report. New York: W. W. Norton, 2004.

Tversky, Amos, and Daniel Kahneman. "The Framing of a Decision on the Psychology of Choice." *Science* 211 (January 1981).

Wayne, Stephen J. "Presidential Bush Goes to War: A Psychological Interpretation from a Distance." In *The Political Psychology of the Gulf War*, edited by Stanley A. Renshon. Pittsburgh, PA: University of Pittsburgh Press, 1993.

Weinberger, Casper. *Fighting for Peace. Seven Critical Years in the Pentagon.* New York: Warner Books, 1990.

Weisman, Steven R. "Pre-emption Evolves From an Idea to Official Action." *The New York Times*, March 22, 2004.

West, James. "Heading for Trouble." *The Washington Post*, September 4, 2002.

Whitehead, Laurence. "The Imposition of Democracy." *In Exporting Democracy The United States and Latin America: Case Studies*, edited by Abraham Lowenthal. Baltimore: Johns Hopkins University Press, 1991.

Williams, Walter. "Bush's Decision Defined by Ideology." *Seattle Post—Intelligencer*, September 28, 2004.

Woodward, Bob. *Plan of Attack.* New York: Simon and Schuster, 2004.

———. "Decision Iraq: Would John Kerry Have Done Things Differently?" *The Washington Post*, October 24, 2004.

———. *Bush at War.* New York: Simon and Schuster, 2002.

———. *The Commanders.* New York: Simon and Schuster, 1991.

Yetiv, Steve A. *The Persian Gulf Crisis.* Westport, CT: Greenwood Press, 1997.

Zagare, Frank C. "Rationality and Deterrence." *World Politics* 42, no. 2 (January 1990).

INDEX

Using this index:

While this book uses a variety of elements to advance its case, at its core is the story and analysis of the decision-makers involved in the United States's dealings with Iraq. Accordingly, this index is divided into two parts. Part I contains the terms found in a regular index. In this section, however, the names of people are omitted. A consolidated list of the leaders, decision-makers, and analysts discussed in this book appears in Part II.